The only behaviour you control is your own

First Edition

First printed in the United Kingdom by TJ International Ltd, Padstow, Cornwall

Published by MemoryBooks

ISBN 978 1 9163903 0 0

Cover design and layout by www.spiffingcovers.com

Published by
MemoryBooks

The only behaviour you control is your own

Martin Humphries

Acknowledgements

Thanks, Dad, for being so principled.

Thanks, Mum, for your love of language.

Thanks, Kim and Tom, for being so rewarding.

Thanks to all those people I have met who have shared their time and wisdom.

Thanks, Jenny, for tolerating me.

Contents

About the Author

Martin Humphries is a man familiar with bad behaviour; his own (at times) and that of his children (at times). He has encountered the bad behaviour of his father, his pupils and work colleagues, the girl on the checkout at the petrol station, and the guy who cut him up at the traffic lights last Friday. And as for that idiot from Accounts…

We all do it, don't we? We all judge other people's behaviour based on our own, because we're so much smarter, kinder, politer than they are… So what do we do? We go right in with the view that it is they who must change to make our life better, not we ourselves.

Martin spent 14 years teaching English to 11-18-year-olds in a comprehensive school in Sheffield with 2,300 pupils, before travelling the world writing and implementing training programmes for the UK's largest training company. Witnessing human behaviour in all its manifestations, contexts and cultures, and noticing his own within the immensely diverse settings he encountered, drove him to sit down and write *The Only Behaviour You Control is Your Own.* It changed his life. He hopes it will change yours.

He now lives in Devon with his wife. He has two children and four grandchildren.

PREAMBLE

The genesis of this book developed from dealing with my father, who was an alcoholic. I was in my forties, and this gruelling experience taught me that it didn't matter what I did or threatened to do, it made absolutely no difference to my father's behaviour. One day I realised that change would only come about if *he* addressed the issue, and it was at that moment I stopped trying to change him. There is a happy ending to this story, thankfully, because my father did visit a psychiatrist. He never spoke about the encounter, but he also never drank again. And after seeing the change in his behaviour, I never drank again in his company.

This whole experience taught me that I, too, needed to look at my own behaviour and, if necessary, make changes. Running a unit for highly disruptive pupils also cemented my belief that it was only by focussing on my own behaviour that any real change would happen, and that how I behaved had a huge influence on those around me.

This is exactly what this book is about. It's about behavioural development, starting with *our own* attitudes and actions. It's about making a change in our behaviour to inspire others.

But as I began writing this book – something I've

always wanted to do – I found myself full of trepidation and self-doubt. Why? Because over the years I'd developed a number of limiting self-beliefs about what I can and what I can't do, and these negative beliefs affected my actions. I've been fortunate in that I've met a lot of amazing people in my life, and shared all sorts of experiences with them; but I've also met people who have created a very toxic atmosphere, and sometimes I've become embroiled in that toxicity, and it changed the way I viewed myself. I wish I'd known back then that instead of trying to change the behaviour of those toxic people, the only behaviour I needed to address was my own. I'm now very conscious, every minute of every hour of every day, of my personal behaviour and, by extension, the influence I have on the people and situations I encounter.

But the reality is, focussing on our own behaviour, and what we're going to do or say in any moment, is a challenge for everyone, no matter what our personal or professional circumstances. We've all been in situations where we've not responded the way we should have, or had people react to us in a way we did not expect – and if, like me, you have an elephant-style memory, it can be difficult to forgive this unexpected behaviour, let alone forget it.

So how do we learn to process behaviour, ours and those around us, in the moment it is happening and decide what we will do or say in response? In my experience, the people who have developed a certain level of conscious attention to behaviour are able to choose their responses wisely. It has been my ambition to do the same; to use my senses to understand and process behaviour, my own included, sometimes in a split-second. It's what we all do naturally, anyway, but not always in a good way.

Learning that the only behaviour we control is our own is the first step to meeting life's challenges without destructive reactions or limiting judgements, whoever we are; and making sure our responses are not from previously learnt behaviour will ensure our behaviour is for the good of those people, and ourselves.

Chapter 1

What Exactly Makes Our Behaviour?

"You cannot control someone else's behaviour.
You can only control your own reaction."
– Anonymous

Despite the fact that we live in a global economy, we often assume we are alike, and yet our life experiences are very different. The resultant differences are because of cross-cultural divides, which can create barriers and misunderstandings in terms of beliefs and values. How often have you heard or engaged in the nature versus nurture debate to try and understand the multiple influences on our behaviour?

But actually it's a lot more complex than simply nature or nurture, because there are more than just the obvious influences on our behaviour. Our behaviour is unique to us because it is influenced by our personal experiences, education, interests, knowledge, social motivation, character, upbringing, values and beliefs.

There are some schools of thought that believe we are not capable of changing our behaviour, or that there are only a limited number of years in our upbringing which form our behaviour. Scientifically speaking, that's not possible. Why?

Because, as we continue to age, our behaviour continues to evolve; and, as we evolve, our lifestyle and preferences also change, thus influencing our behaviour.

Another huge influence is social media, and we are only just beginning to understand its influence on behaviour, and how people connect and react to each other, often without ever meeting. I think it would be true to say that social media is perhaps one of the biggest factors that influences our behaviour in the 21st century.

Why We Need to Look at Behaviour

Now more than ever, we need to invest a great deal of energy into analysing how we behave in certain situations, not just in our personal lives but in our professional lives too. We need to look at the personal development of our children, and educate them in how to monitor their behaviour, how to approach different relationships, how to be genuine, and to take responsibility. They, too, need to learn to question things, and themselves, and learn the power of behaviour.

We can all refine our behaviour and not let others define us, which is one of the most priceless lessons we can learn in life. This lesson helps us to take control of our behaviour, because it puts us in a position whereby we can influence the people around us *without trying to change them directly.* In turn, this influence will hopefully help them strive to become a better, or the best version, of themselves.

This book shares the many ways we can develop on a personal level, and emphasises the fact that we need to give up trying to control the behaviour and thoughts of other people. The simple truth is, we can't change them; but we can shape our behaviour so they might take inspiration from it, and, if necessary, take a look at their own.

One of the skills we all need to develop is the ability to reflect each other's behaviour. What does this mean? If we imagine we are a mirror, we realise we have the power to reflect how other people are behaving right back at them. But this works both ways, as when we imagine they, too, are a mirror, we get to see how we are behaving, and how that looks. We also need to look at *how* we are communicating, not just through our words but through our tone of voice and body language.

An example of this, is how we greet each other. When we meet someone we often ask how they are. Usually, however, we ask this out of common courtesy, not because we are particularly interested in how they are doing. And it's easy to spot when someone asks us this question and we sense they don't actually care if we are OK. If we are to influence how others behave in this respect, we must first look at ourselves. What is our body language saying when we ask this question? Are we making eye contact or looking over someone's shoulder? Is our tone of voice warm or disinterested? We have a vast range of tools in our communication armoury which we can use skilfully in this situation, and really make a difference. Try it. Try greeting someone with a warm smile, good eye contact and genuine interest. It may not work immediately, but soon it will be noticed, and it will most likely have a remarkable effect on that person, and we too may soon be greeted with a smile and a genuine inquiry about how we are. *This is the mirror at work.*

Are You Proud of Your Behaviour?

It's entirely up to us how we behave; and it's entirely up to us to become the person we are proud of. But that means taking absolute responsibility for who we are, and our thoughts and actions.

If something goes wrong in our life, or we don't like something, how often do we blame anyone but ourselves? How often do we hear the local council being blamed for the amount of litter around, for instance? Is litter really their responsibility alone? Are we not, as individuals in a community, responsible at all? This is an example of how our behaviour can influence a situation. Instead of moaning about a newspaper blowing across the street on a windy day, pick it up and put it back in the recycling bin. Not everyone will follow suit, but some will. And certainly there will be children watching, for whom this is an excellent example of having pride in our community – and ourselves. No one loses if we take positive action rather than assigning blame and walking on by.

Every situation is an opportunity to analyse our own reactions and behaviour. This is a much more effective way of thinking, and it is empowering to take responsibility in this way, asking ourselves if there is anything we can learn from a situation, if there is anything we could do differently, for a different outcome.

If we try to change someone else's behaviour, our

attempts will rarely get the results we want. So instead of wasting our time and energy, focus on our own behaviour, and the outcome will be better.

We are the only one in charge of our minds, and our reactions. The mass media, social media, the opinions of our friends down the pub – these things all try to make us think or act in a certain way; but in the end it is we who have a choice whether to listen and be influenced or not. Therefore, we are also in charge of whether we get the desired results in life or not.

Remembering this means we can overcome our weaknesses, claim our own power, become assertive, and influence the behaviour of other people – and be proud of the person we are.

Be the Guide, Not the Bully

Interestingly, the only time we are able to change someone's behaviour is when they are a baby, or a small child, and even then it is not always plain sailing, as very quickly a child will learn the word NO! and seek ways to do things their way. As teenagers, this is even more apparent, and more than ever we must learn to lead by example rather than force. As a matter of fact, forcing people to change their behaviour will only create stress between you.

The problem most people face is when they want to impose good qualities on others, and their efforts are rejected. But we cannot cajole another person into changing their habits; they will only change if they want to. We cannot make a teenager study harder; they will study when they want to. And making threats or offering bribes is futile, and may cause resentment in the long term, and in fact doesn't encourage a person to look at themselves, for themselves. The only thing we can do is take impeccable care of our behaviour and lead by example.

When we lead by example we make the whole process of influencing other people a whole lot easier, interesting, and appealing. Showing instead of telling is a great way to influence people.

When we are in a relationship, for instance, and see something that irritates us, what can we do to avoid 'telling' and instead 'show' what it is we would like to change? Sometimes all it takes is for us to do something differently – like always saying please and thank you when someone does something for us – to change the behaviour and habits of others in our household.

Why is it we tend to notice what other people are doing rather than what we are doing? Again, this comes back to the mirror. The Swiss psychiatrist Carl Jung said, "*Everything that irritates us about others can lead us to an understanding of ourselves*." Nothing could be truer.

In our relationships, personal and professional, we will always encounter things that irritate us. Have a look at why. Is the irritation more about us than about them? If we honestly believe it's about the other person, then we must still steer clear of going in and trying to change them. The only thing we can change is our own reaction; and the only thing we can do is perhaps share information with them, in the hope that they might open up their mind to some sort of new perspective on the matter. But the effect will almost certainly be limited. Why? Because only they can change themselves. We cannot change them.

As an example, a friend of mine was in a house share with a guy who left the lights on in every room. It didn't matter how many times my friend asked him, or yelled at him to turn them off when he left the room, he still left them on. We had a conversation about this. I asked him what it was that made him so angry specifically. Was it the fact that Will left the lights on, or was it that Will wasn't like him, super-efficient and aware of the cost both financially and environmentally of leaving all the lights on? He laughed, and then admitted it was so much more about him rather than his housemate's forgetfulness. The brilliant outcome was, when my friend stopped bullying Will about the lights and left a few on himself, Will started turning them off!

Trying to make someone change only causes suffering, to some degree or another, and creates tension and stress. Better then to consider what the Bible advises: "*Why do you look at the speck of sawdust in your brother's eye and pay no attention to the plank in your own eye*?" (Matthew 7:3. New International Version).

Bad Reactions versus Good Responses

Some of us, we love the idea of changing other people, and spend excessive amounts of time and energy trying to do just that, getting angry, upset or frustrated if they don't change.

But why should we believe we have the power to

change the behaviour of another person, who is just as independent as we are? Come to think of it, just the thought of being able to change someone is outright ridiculous. Think about how difficult we find it to change our own behaviour!

So why do we do it? It might be because we like to exert some sort of power over people, or because we think our way is the only right way, or maybe because we think we are the decision-makers, and have a right to inflict our opinion on people. And when we don't get the response we'd like, we take to asking, *How could he/she say such a thing?* or *How can he/she be so rude?* or *Why would he/she do that?*

We react that way because our emotions are affected by other people's opinions and decisions, particularly if they are very different to our own; and, consequently, we react emotionally, rather than in a rational or a logical manner, which makes things ten times worse.

There's no magic involved in stopping trying to control or change other people's behaviour, or reacting badly in situations where we should have controlled our emotions. All we need to do is reflect upon *our own* thoughts.

We can do this in the moment, if possible, or we can write them down and review them. For instance, when we find ourselves thinking something like, *I wish he/she wouldn't do that,* or *I can't believe he/she thinks that,* notice these thoughts. This allows us to pause our automatic reactions, which might not be for the good, and put us in charge of our own behaviour. The outcome of taking time to formulate a more rational response can make the difference between collapse of a conversation and the resultant frustration or anger, or the continuance of the discussion and the ability to resolve the issue. If we can't do it in the moment, then agreeing to pick up the conversation at another time, and getting into the habit of writing down how we feel, will ensure we go back to a thing with clarity and calm. So much better for everyone!

People often spend weeks, months and, at times, years in psychotherapy trying to change their behaviour or thoughts. That's because such changes often take considerable time to implement. Sometimes behaviour is not changed at all, even if the person wanted it to be, because sadly old behaviour patterns are so engrained. Most of us, though, we can succeed in changing our thoughts and reactions. And when we do, we find ourselves living happier and much more peaceful lives.

Instant Judgements and Behaviour

Some people call themselves 'people watchers', but this is something we all do, if we're honest, and we will often make judgements based on our observations. For instance, how people dress or their body language will influence our perception of an individual. If they speak a different language, or have an accent, this may lead us to stereotype the person, or even make instant negative judgements. We seem to carry around in our heads a checklist by which we measure a person, without actually knowing a single thing about them other than what they're wearing, how they walk, or how they speak. Why is that? And why does it instantly affect how we behave around them?

If we are to master our thoughts and behaviour, we need to analyse these perceptions and judgements, because we can be pretty sure if we're judging them, they may be judging us, and that, without a doubt, changes the way we behave around each other. Approaching a person without that judgement – being in control of our own behaviour, in other words – changes our exchange and connection with that individual, which in turn may change theirs towards us.

Chapter 2

Personal Growth

"I want to grow. I want to be better. You grow. We all grow. We're made to grow. You either evolve or you disappear."
– Tupac Shakur

A simple way of explaining personal growth is 'working on ourselves', making ourselves a better version of who we are, bringing out the best in who we can be. Personal growth is all about developing personal skills, too, and expanding our horizons, our influence and our capabilities.

Growing on a personal level is absolutely essential. Jim Rohn, a great speaker, said, "W*ork on yourself harder than you do on your job.*" Working on ourselves means we become far more capable professionally and personally, which, as a consequence, makes us far more valuable to the marketplace, and able to make a success of many areas of business.

Engaging in personal development has the power to take us from wherever we are currently standing to wherever we want to be in the world. It doesn't really matter where we are from, or what our background is, personal development is the path to success. It's a great way to raise our consciousness, and make us more present and aware, which means we can enjoy life to the fullest and say goodbye to low vibrational thoughts and negative thinking.

Personal growth can make us stand out in a crowd as a positive influence, someone whose thoughts and actions are for the good.

There is no right or wrong amount of time we should commit to personal development on a daily basis, just the attention we give ourselves with the intention of improving, even if it's just for a few moments.

You might be wondering how to pursue personal growth? There is no one ideal way to grow on a personal level. The process is unique for every person. Some of us might prefer reading books; others might listen to audio books or podcasts; some like to attend courses or seminars. In truth, anything that grows and expands our consciousness and awareness is beneficial. And we can do this for general growth as well as specific growth, such as developing confidence as a public speaker or when negotiating deals, or re-entering the workplace after a break, such as maternity leave or raising small children.

There are so many things we can do, even getting involved in a sport we haven't tried before, or learning to play an instrument. We could also visit new places, or open ourselves up to experiences that are new to us. For instance, if we say we don't like or understand classical music, go to a concert, see how it feels. In short, we can do anything that expands who we are and makes us look at our place in our life and our behaviour with those we meet.

There are so many situations that present an

opportunity for personal growth, but here we're going to look at choice, challenges and crisis.

Choice and Personal Growth

"One can choose to go back toward safety or forward toward growth. Growth must be chosen again and again; fear must be overcome again and again."
– ABRAHAM H. MASLOW

Life offers us many chances to make a choice; but sometimes it's not about taking the easy option. Sometimes personal choice involves pain and sacrifice, for instance choosing to spend time with someone who is sick, or depressed. But this has a twofold benefit, as the person we spend that time with feels cared for, and we are able to develop a side of ourselves we may not be familiar or comfortable with. Personal growth under any circumstances is never wasted, and will never be cause for regret.

Such choices are an investment in ourselves, and they draw us closer to the kind of person we want to be, becoming the barometer by which we can navigate our lives. Avoiding making choices like these can create difficulties later on, when we realise we do not have the tools to cope with a situation.

*"It's your choice how to respond to challenges,
how to live in the moment, and whether you will
fight for excellence in everything you do."*
– Charlie Harary, from
*Unlocking Greatness: The Unexpected Journey
from the Life You Have to the Life You Want.*

Our choices have a long-lasting effect on our lives. Dedication to personal growth often means making the difficult choices, not just the easy ones.

Choice and the Matter of Risk

When making a choice, we could ask ourselves the following questions:

- Will I regret this decision?
- Does this decision uphold my values and integrity?
- What will I gain if I make this decision?
- What could I lose if I make this decision?

Making a choice that will lead to personal growth often means stepping out of our comfort zone. It may also mean feeling uncomfortable or embarrassed in front of our peers, family and friends. These are not things which we should let get in our way. But what if risk is involved?

Choosing to do something which involves taking risks may conflict with our usual behaviour, and this is where we must decide whether the risk is of long-term use to us, or is simply taking a risk for the sake of it.

For example, we may decide we want to climb Kilimanjaro as part of our personal growth. This may be something way out of our comfort zone, and might seem like a good way to challenge that zone; but if we have a young family, or a health issue, is this really a good choice?

We must consider the ripple effect, therefore, and look at how that choice might affect the lives of others, and ourselves.

Choice and Shortcuts

"All growth depends upon activity.
There is no development physically or intellectually
without effort, and effort means work."
– Calvin Coolidge

There's no denying the fact that we all look for shortcuts, whether in business, finances or relationships. The craving for success may compel us to make bad choices: we shake on a deal without looking at the small print; we take on a huge loan to fund the life we think we should have; we pay little attention to our relationship, yet expect it to flourish.

To take the example of a relationship, if we want it to last we need to put the other person's interests before our own, be a good listener and take time to nurture that relationship. We might be tempted to think, *Well, what's in that for me*? The truth is, everything! Because by investing time and attention in our partner, we strengthen our own development as well as the relationship. No shortcut ever led to long-lasting growth; it's just the quick fix that quickly fades to nothing.

If we want to grow on a personal level, and professionally, we must put the work in, because that's what will carry us on into the future.

Challenges and Personal Growth

Here's a little food for thought: If you want to improve who you are, how would you feel about a healthy dose of discomfort and challenge in life to drive that personal growth? As it turns out, breaking a habit, taking a (calculated) risk, trying something exciting and new, making new acquaintances, and putting yourself in a completely new situation might be just what we need. It might not be easy, and it could be exhausting, but the rewards are amazing.

The thing with comfort is that it can lead to boredom, discontent and self-absorption; and when it comes to either being comfortable or stretching ourselves and growing, try choosing the latter, because accepting challenges in life teaches us so much more than sitting doing nothing.

"People who regularly seek out fresh experiences tend to be more creative and emotionally resilient than those who remain stuck in routine. Breaking your own mould can only make you stronger and more confident to reach higher levels in your professional and personal life."

– Dr Elizabeth Lombardo, psychologist and author of *Better than Perfect*

We cannot grow into better versions of ourselves if we keep avoiding discomfort. Therefore, the sooner we learn to embrace discomfort, the better our growth will be. However, the transition will be uncomfortable and somewhat scary, but that's how we learn. Discomfort is a catalyst for personal growth; it pushes us to our limits and forces us to change and adapt; it demands that we become more than what we currently are by creating new perspectives, acquiring new skills, and pushing personal boundaries in order to overcome the obstacles we're facing. All of this amounts to personal growth.

There are all sorts of obstacles to deal with in life. Maybe a harsh boss, who makes your job more difficult; maybe argumentative co-workers who affect your productivity; or perhaps a competitive rival who has made your life a living hell. The big thing here is: we must not avoid difficult people if we want to achieve success, because it turns out that being in the company of difficult people stimulates growth in our life.

No matter what the shape and size of discomfort we encounter in life, we must learn to live comfortably with the discomfort. This is perhaps the most important skill we will get to learn in life. Why? Because if we master discomfort, we can master just about anything.

Getting out of your comfort zone every once in a while challenges your mental skills, making you better able to deal with the discomfort. As a result, we end up beating procrastination, developing a new habit, learning a new language, speaking on stage, exploring new things, and making it through physically and mentally gruelling events.

Do this and you will never feel more alive.

Some things seem impossible until they are done. Thus, it may be time to tackle the fear that has kept you from growing and progressing in life.

"Don't limit your challenges;
challenge your limits."
– Jerry Dunn

What Jerry Dunn says is so true, because we all possess the ability to rise to a challenge, and the rewards in terms of personal growth are so worth it. All we have to do is get uncomfortable for a while. How? By pushing ourselves to learn something new, permitting ourselves to think and act beyond our usual remit, and stepping up to do something when we don't feel like doing it. Every time we do, we get more in charge of our behaviour, and better able to deal with what life chucks our way.

Crisis and Personal Growth

A crisis can occur in our life in an instant. One moment, we're feeling happy and content; the next it feels as if the ground beneath our feet has disappeared. It could be the loss of our job, the end of a serious relationship, a health issue, the passing of someone dearly loved, or a physical injury. And there's no doubt these things can turn your life upside down.

I defy anybody to watch the Paralympic Games and not marvel at the sheer grit, determination and perseverance of those who have overcome debilitating physical conditions to compete at Olympic level. I find it humbling, and I am full of admiration.

The reality is, we're all so busy trying to keep up with the daily demands of life that we don't give much thought to our ability to deal with serious problems until we actually face one. But that's not the only reason we're ill-equipped to manage a crisis. There's always an element of avoidance; and we avoid preparing ourselves for the serious stuff because we don't really want to think about it. True?

"Start shaping your own life. This journey is yours, take charge of it. Stop letting your life be shaped by fate, circumstances and the whims of others."

– Marquita Herald

It's also true that it's difficult to prepare, because a) we don't want to spend our time dwelling on the what-ifs, and b) we have no idea what the what-ifs might be. However, we need to be ready enough to decide what to do next if anything drastic should happen. For instance, if we lose our job, considering what we might do should this happen immediately presents us with choices we have already thought about: we can either see ourselves as a victim, or take advantage of the opportunity and find a job we've always wanted to do. Being able to see the opportunities in a crisis means we have a better chance of using it for personal growth.

There are several things we can do if we choose to view crisis as an opportunity for growth.

1. Face the Reality

Denying the effects of the crisis only keeps you from confronting the new reality; and repressing your feelings will also not do you any good, because they'll just resurface with more intensity whenever you go through a similar crisis again. The only way to survive is to push through the pain and grow, accepting the reality and channelling all your anger and pain in a healthy way.

2. Take Action

When going through a personal crisis, you may not feel like mapping out what happens next. However, assessing your options and planning small steps can restore the feeling of stability and control in your life. Clinging to anything familiar and safe might feel like the easier option, but new opportunities can be missed if you do so. Opening your mind to different possibilities when your world has just turned upside down makes such a difference.

3. Avoid Self-pity

There's no emotion more insidious than self-pity. It can quickly overwhelm you, however, when you're trying to manage a crisis; and you cannot help but feel that somehow you should have been able to prevent the situation you are now in. An essential part of growing through a crisis is accepting that pain in life is inevitable, but suffering is optional. This keeps you from pitying yourself in a crisis. Self-pity is a very addictive emotion, so whether you opt for moving forward or drowning yourself in suffering is a choice only you can make.

4. Talk it Through

Talking the crisis through with others helps relieve the burden, and makes you realise you're not the only one going through a difficult time. Talking to someone also provides a different perspective. If you can't find anyone who will listen to you, or who you feel comfortable talking to, write it all down. Writing down how you feel and what thoughts are consuming your mind is a therapy that, without a shadow of doubt, helps you grow through the crisis and out the other side.

"Don't waste time on mental reruns about what you could (should, would) have done differently. Just because you've hit a few rough spots on your journey, doesn't mean your future can't be better than you ever imagined."

– Anonymous

5. Learn to Trust Others Again

It's normal to feel vulnerable and insecure when the crisis might be a betrayal, either personal or professional. When a relationship with someone you love has broken down, or when a friendship ends, or when you lose a job you invested your heart in, it's difficult to trust anyone or anything again. To restore confidence in the people around you is perhaps the most difficult part of recovering from a crisis of this nature, because you want to avoid future hurt. However, you can't continue to live without trust, and a huge part of personal growth is learning to trust again. The reward of getting over this fear is a life well-lived.

Perhaps we are someone who keeps on having the same bad experiences over and over again – and I'm not talking about the unexpected events, but a repeating pattern of getting fired, or breaking up with a partner, for example? It could be we're unlucky; but more likely it's because we're not learning the lessons needed and are missing out on the opportunities for personal growth, and the subsequent change in our behaviour.

Indeed, a personal crisis can be a blessing in disguise, provided we are happy to learn lessons from it. Life's lessons are tough, but each one of them holds the opportunity for growth, helping us to understand our strengths and weaknesses, and making it possible for us to regain forward momentum. We alone have the power to make the change for the better.

"The pain you feel today is the strength
you feel tomorrow. For every challenge encountered
there is an opportunity for growth."

– Anonymous

CHAPTER 3

Uniqueness

"People undergo several sequential steps in maturing from infancy, including childhood, adolescences, young adulthood, middle age, and old age. Each stage presents distinct challenges that require a person to amend how they think and act. The motive for seeking significant change in a person's manner of perceiving the world and behaving vary. Alteration of a person's mindset can commence with a growing sense of awareness that a person is dissatisfied with an aspect of his or her life, which cause a person consciously to consider amending their lifestyle."

– KILROY J. OLDSTER

It's important to understand several elements, which, when combined, affect the way we interact and behave in our personal and professional space.

We all know that our behaviour is a manifestation of the unique environments we have all grown up in, which comprise different experiences, beliefs and interests. For instance, if we grew up in an environment where our parents yelled at each other, and us, when they weren't happy about something, the chances are we will also end up yelling to express ourselves when we're confronted with something that annoys us. We are also influenced by the behaviour of other people we meet, and the company we keep.

Our immediate environment is an integral piece of the puzzle when we look at our behaviour, but that does not mean we are predestined for a particular behaviour. Genetics have a part in the puzzle too, because it's true that we do inherit certain personality traits from our parents. So we have two choices, as we can't just turn our genes off at will, and sometimes are unable to remove ourselves from our current environment: we can either stick with what we know, or explore other ways to behave, which involves looking at various aspects of our personalities, like our moods, habits and attitudes. When we learn to recognise these in ourselves, then we can start to change the bits that are not serving us.

1. Moods

It's normal to experience mood swings through all the various phases and cycles of life, like puberty for instance. Stress and anxiety can also cause a change in mood. Sometimes there is a rush of anger, or sadness. Sometimes we just want to be alone. The one thing we need to understand about mood swings is that they are temporary, and should not have a long-term impact. (If they linger, and are having a serious impact, this could be indicative of something more serious and we should seek help.)

It is not the responsibility of other people to cope with our mood swings; it is *we* who need to be in control of our emotions. It's important, then, to look at why the mood swings are happening, and what we can do about them.

Mood swings can be hormonal, or they can be triggered by bad diet, or bad habits, like not getting enough sleep or frequently arriving at work with a hangover, for instance. Most of these can be managed by looking at what you eat: a high-sugar diet will make you prone to extreme highs and lows, making you either excitable or grumpy; and the effects of a lack of sleep are well documented. Adolescence is a difficult time with hormones, and women are susceptible to a lifetime of hormone fluctuations which can greatly affect their mood.

Someone in the throes of a mood swing may lose their temper, or become aggressive for no apparent reason. Conversely, they might go quiet, appear depressed, or lack enthusiasm or energy.

There are two issues here: someone else's mood swings, and our own, and what to do in both cases.

Personally, we can help neutralise mood swings by noticing them, and by keeping a record of when they occur and why. Do we need to change to a healthier diet, get sufficient sleep, start exercising more? If we notice a certain situation alters our mood, look at why. Is it because we find it stressful, tiring or challenging? Keeping track of all these elements will help us to manage them, change things that need changing – like diet or our mental approach to a stressful situation, for instance – and ultimately change our behaviour. If anything is unmanageable, then perhaps it is time to seek help. There is no shame in that.

If it is someone else's mood swings that are affecting us, what can we do? It's certainly not easy to cope with, but 'meeting fire with fire' – or reacting in a similar manner – is not going to help. Better to show empathy; maybe talk to the person when they are ready, and ask if there's anything we can do to help. This is our behaviour being a force for good, rather than making a situation worse.

2. Habits

We all have a set of habits that shape our entire day, even our life. And whether good or bad, they actually shape our entire personality, too. Even the simplest habit of brushing our teeth first thing in the morning and before we go to bed at night, or always holding a door open for someone, is an indication of who we are.

Thus, habits play a vital role in presenting who you are in the eyes of people who surround you, whether in your personal sphere or at your workplace. Good habits generally equal a healthier and happier life, of that there is no doubt.

We possibly don't need to go into what bad habits do for our lives, as we're all aware of how they can make us feel, and how they affect our energy and quality of life.

We all have the option to adopt healthy and constructive habits which improve our lives. And it's incredible the things we notice when we do. The improvement of our mood, our general sense of wellbeing, and how much energy we have definitely make a difference to how we feel we are evolving as human being.

They say old habits die hard. But this applies to both bad and good habits. Only we know which habits we want to die.

3. Attitudes

Ever heard the expression, 'You have a real attitude problem'? Our attitude affects how we feel about every single situation and person in our life; and what we choose to do or not do is the direct result of our attitude. It's our attitude that drives reaction from other people, too.

Let's say we have a very positive and joyful attitude. If we project that attitude, we are far more likely to attract positive experiences and interactions. If we have a negative attitude, however, fuelled by 'poor me' or 'why does bad stuff always happen to me?' we're going to attract more bad stuff, unfortunately.

A positive attitude breeds optimism in our lives. It allows us to cope with our daily affairs more easily. Day-to-day challenges don't worry us so much, and we generally come up with better ways to manage them. With a positive attitude, we feel brighter, more creative, and more ready to face life head on.

The following exercises really help in keeping our attitude positive:

- We are not our thoughts. Let all the negative feelings and thoughts we experience in a day just pass by. No good can come out of these feelings, so why give them any attention?
- Direct thoughts towards positive things and expect good things to happen. They almost certainly will.
- Believe in success, whatever it is we are doing. Build

that kind of faith in ourselves.

- If something goes wrong, analyse why it went wrong, and learn from it rather than going down the 'poor me' route.
- Mistakes and problems are opportunities in disguise, not a reason to throw the towel in.
- Show up with a positive attitude, whatever the situation.

There's no denying that a positive attitude can become a strong characteristic of our behaviour and a sure way of inspiring people around us. It's also essential for living a fulfilling and enjoyable life. The more we practice projecting a positive attitude in our life, the more we realise the value of it. It vastly improves both our personal and professional life; it helps us to become a person known for our inspiring behaviour.

4. Values

First off, we need to understand what values are. Values are customs, ideals or standards we choose to live by; they are the things we really believe in, and are the drivers for our behaviour. For instance, most people consider a monogamous life the norm; but some people believe that you gain status or prestige if you live a polygamous life. The point to focus on here is that a certain value may be seen as good or acceptable by one group of people, whereas another group or culture may think a particular value is bad or unacceptable – and this directly affects behaviour, not only within the group, but towards each other.

Considering that we all have our own unique set of values, what should we do if we disagree with someone else's customs or beliefs? The bottom line is, if we expect others to respect our values and not hurt us, we should reciprocate, as long as those values don't hurt anyone else. That's what makes our behaviour an inspiration for others.

5. Personality

Our personality is defined by our typical pattern of thinking, feeling, acting and communicating; it is also defined by how we behave, not just with one person or group of people we are familiar with, but with people in general. Think of a person who, in your opinion, has a personality you admire, and then identify the characteristics of this person's personality and why they appeal. Perhaps they are kind, a good listener, or hard working? Or maybe they are a good leader, someone who sees the best in people and is always encouraging?

There are so many factors and variables that go into making up somebody's individual personality. Taking a look at traits we admire in others can help us to develop similar traits in ourselves. For instance:

- **Be a better listener.** We could work on our active listening skills, because when we're listening to somebody, it's not just our ears that are involved in the process; our whole body should be listening, too, which means putting our phone away, nodding, and maintaining eye contact.
- **Be interested in people.** By experiencing new things ourselves, we will find more in common with those we

meet; but conversely, not experiencing a thing should not make us tune out, but tune in when people are sharing their experiences. Tuning in means we will learn something, and makes the person feel valued when we thank them for telling us.

- **Stay optimistic about life.** Avoiding being pessimistic and talking about things in a negative way makes all the difference not just to our own day, but for those around us.
- **Be encouraging and supportive.** Raise people up with positive energy and encouraging comments. Be the one who says, 'You did a great job with that' or 'How can I help?' if someone looks like they're struggling.
- **Have integrity.** This means being true to our word. Don't be the sort of person who says one thing and does another. This damages people's trust in us, and trust is difficult to rebuild.
- **Treat people with respect.** Don't talk badly of people or make fun of them behind their back. People who gossip are not very highly regarded, and breed mistrust.
- **Accept your faults.** This is something all great personalities have in common. None of us is perfect. When we get something wrong, or discover we've annoyed someone, don't get all defensive, accept it and move on.

Shaping our personality into something we admire is never going to be a bad thing, and will help us maintain behaviour we can be proud of.

6. Temperament

Numerous people suffer from temperament issues, and an inability to manage our anger or temper can lead to serious troubles in our lives. It can cost us our job, our relationships, our friendships and, ultimately, our self-respect.

Hurtful, aggressive words that are said without thinking cannot be retracted and do great harm. And as for physical aggression… The key to a calm and enjoyable life is learning to control the impulse to lose the plot and attack someone, verbally or otherwise. There are better ways to channel that rush of energy that leads to throwing things around, shouting, cursing and punching walls.

The reality is, our inability to handle situations calmly does more damage than we realise. Besides affecting our heart and weakening our immune system, a foul temper can actually trigger anxiety and even depression, as its consequences are often broken relationships, friendships and trust. In short, a whole lot of heartbreak.

If you feel the pressures of life are getting too much, and your anger is getting the better of you, and taking a toll on your health and relationships, it's time to learn to manage it before it's too late.

Losing our temper is an emotional not a rational response to difficulties. Here are some ideas on noticing our anger, and what to do:

- Identify what situations and circumstances make us lose our temper. Once we do that, we can try to avoid getting into those situations. There are some situations in life which we can't completely avoid, however, like someone cutting us up at a junction, or a work colleague who always winds us up, but the moment we start to get intensely angry, look at it, let it go. It's simply not worth it.

- Relaxation techniques help control our emotions. Counting back from 10 to one, or simply breathing out in long, slow breaths immediately releases tension. This allows us the little bit of time needed to get control.
- Words are very powerful. Pick a mantra or sentence that really works for you and say it over and over in your head. It doesn't matter what it is. Just say it.

It's so hard to bite our tongue sometimes, it's true. But we all know that once the words are out, you can't take them back, and this can have all sorts of repercussions. Thus, showing some restraint while in conversation with someone who always seems to make us feel angry is the kind of behaviour worth developing.

By way of conclusion to this discussion on our personalities and how they affect those around us, here are seven elements which constitute unproductive personal and professional relationships:

- Criticising
- Blaming
- Complaining
- Nagging
- Threatening
- Punishing
- Bribing

And here are four that promote productive relationships:

- Listening
- Encouraging
- Supporting
- Rewarding

In our unique way, and based on our values and attention to who we are, we all get to choose who we actually want to be.

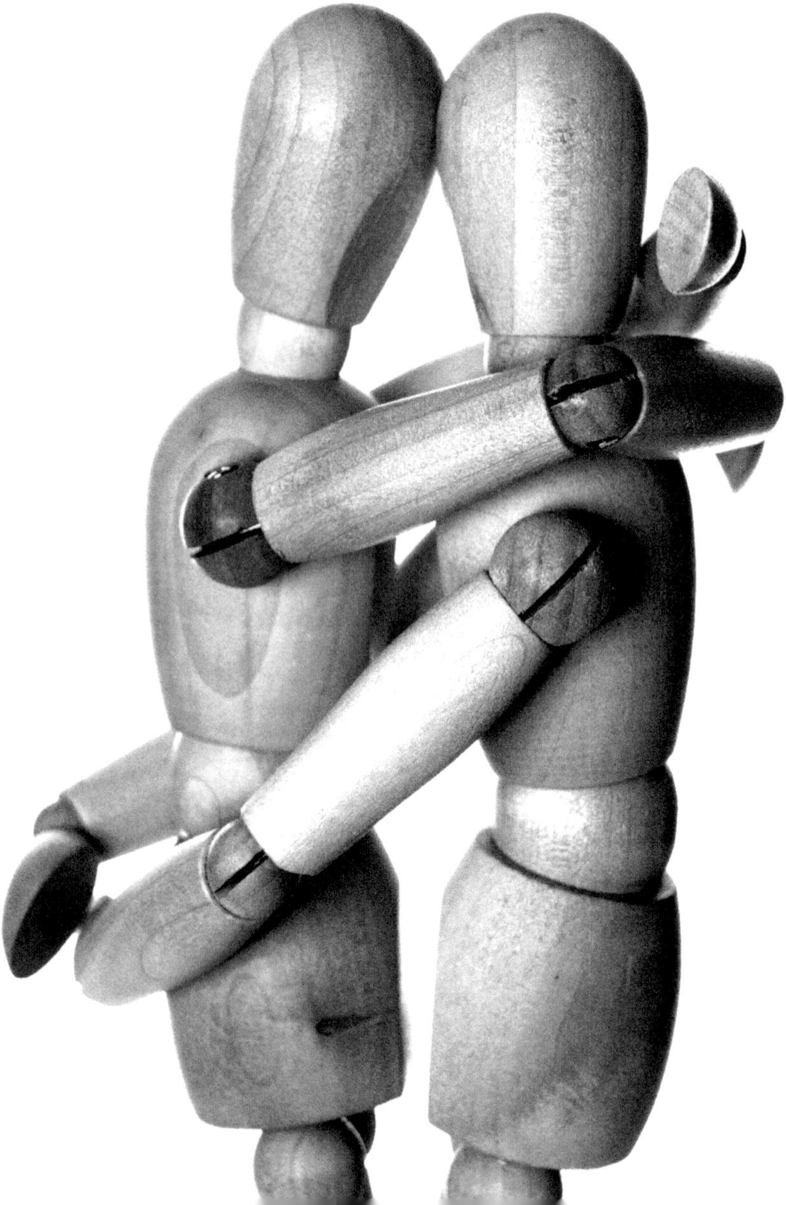

Chapter 4

Relationships

"A great relationship is about two things: first, find out the similarities; second, respect the differences."
– Anonymous

It is important to understand that a relationship, of whatever nature, is incomplete without differences. But how can we accept those differences when they are the complete opposite of our values? This is a seemingly difficult question that a lot of people struggle with, because there cannot be two people who think in exactly the same way, always prefer the same things, and have the same priorities and interests in life.

We can start by differentiating between our values or universal human needs, and what we imagine the other person's values and universal needs to be. One very important thing to keep in mind here is that everything any of us do is driven by one of many human needs, which include the need for love, respect, kindness, home, shelter, food, etc. Therefore, if we break down any person's actions or choices, we realise that it's actually their attempt to get one or more of those needs met.

But people have different ways of expressing those

needs. Some get loud; some go quiet. Both ways are equally as challenging. What about our own needs? How do we go about expressing them? There are many aspects to this discussion, so let's take a look at some of them.

Accepting Differences in Your Relationships

"You don't develop courage by being happy in your relationships every day. You develop it by surviving difficult times and challenging adversity."

– Epicurus

How we deal with differences in our relationships says a lot about our attitude, and is reflected in our behaviour. We can either let our relationship deteriorate, or do our best to overcome the differences. I think we can all say that when we first meet a partner, we can be pretty smitten by their unique personality. In other words, we are attracted to how different they are to us, as well as our similarities. For instance, we may think it's great that our partner is more carefree than we are. However, as time passes, we may come to realise how annoying their lack of concern is; and we might end up wishing our partner was more like us, or they could see things and do things the way we do, and that if they did we would get along so much better than we actually do.

The key is to see differences as something of value, and not as a source of conflict. That's a little easier said than done, it's true, but it is possible. When we accept the fact that differences add value rather than cause conflict, we are often able to save a relationship from falling apart. Here are a few important ways of how to do this:

- Perhaps the most highly recommended way is to talk openly and in detail about how you are different, but always in a spirit of acceptance. It is vital to talk about the **situation** that is the source of the issue, however, not the person's personality, as this will make them defensive and you might end up making the matter worse than it already is.
- Avoid arguing about who has the best way of doing things because this won't solve the problem!
- You could try taking turns doing things the other way, which provides an opportunity to understand why a person does things differently to you.
- Try to see where the difference is coming from by getting to its root cause.
- You could offer to help. For instance, if your partner is always running late, you could ask if there is anything you can do to help him or her arrive on time.
- Try to see the world from your partner's point of view. This means letting go of your ego and learning about your partner's stance on a thing.
- Be patient. Controlling your emotions and temper is the kind of behaviour you want to develop when discussing differences.
- Notice when their different perspective has had a positive impact on you, and tell them.

Two people can be different in countless ways, but if we open all conversations with the end goal of moving the relationship forward, despite the differences, both parties are winners through and through. Accepting differences can enrich our lives and help us develop the capability of doing what is really important: managing our own behaviour.

The Importance of Empathy

Being in a relationship means being there for one another. If that's not the case, it can trigger loneliness, even when we have friends and loved ones in our lives. Feeling lonely in a relationship often occurs because we feel our partner cannot empathise with our values and feelings.

Empathising with others is the prerequisite of making any sort of relationship work; it means, *I can feel that you understand me.* However, owing to the many differences between two people, it's difficult to empathise with another person all the time.

To enjoy a healthy and strong relationship, it's important that we feel deeply connected to each other. If we feel we are losing that connection, practising empathy can help strengthen the emotional bond between you.

But what does being empathetic actually mean? It means being aware of someone's emotions and seeing things from their perspective, just as we would like them to see things from ours. We need to *feel* what the other person feels in order to make our relationship work, not just simply say we understand.

Just to make things clearer, empathy is poles apart from sympathy. According to a licensed marriage and family therapist, Barbara Cunningham, *"Empathy drives connection where sympathy can disempower. Empathy is 'I'm so glad you told me that.' You respect your partner's adulthood without judgement."*

Showing empathy is a testament to a commendable personality. It shows we have the behaviour it takes to make a relationship work. So what aspects of our behaviour show we have the quality to empathise with other people? Whether we use cognitive, emotional or compassionate empathy, is down to personal choice; the point is that empathy in any form creates stronger, more loving relationships.

Put Yourself in Your Partner's Shoes

Showing empathetic behaviour can solidify our relationship because it proves we understand and care for our partner. One way of showing empathy is imagining yourself in your partner's position. According to a New York-based therapist and relationship expert: *"People who lack empathy tend to also lack an understanding of how they themselves feel in varying situations. Therefore, a good starting point is to remind people to consider how they feel as they endure life's mixed bag of good, bad and neutral experiences. This exercise will put down neural pathways (which will be strengthened over time) that allow for a person to understand experience – first his/her own, then that of someone else."*

Try Communicating Your Emotions

Yes, active listening is extremely important in relationships, but communicating your emotions is also equally important.

Developing the habit of telling other people that you know they are going through difficult times is an excellent behavioural feature, and actually makes a world of difference in relationships. It shows you are not dismissing them and can relate to their feelings.

Withhold Your Judgements

The best kind of relationship is the one where everyone involved gets to grow and learn together; but that is only possible when you avoid judging the other person and making them feel small. A person in charge of their own behaviour will withhold judgement of his or her partner's choices, and will assume those choices were made after careful consideration, regardless of whether or not they ultimately lead to success.

Take Some of Your Partner's Responsibilities

A great way of showing empathy is to take on some of your partner's daily chores and responsibilities, thus demonstrating that you care about them and are concerned about his or her wellbeing. Also, it's a great way of determining what your partner goes through every day so you can stop judging.

Take Wants and Needs into Consideration

You need to develop the ability to look past your own perspective. Sometimes it pays to put your partner's needs and wants before yours. This deepens their trust in you, and proves that you care about them.

If we want to develop empathetic behaviour, we could

start by asking ourselves when we last felt really connected to our partner. If we don't feel that way, the chances are they probably feel the same, and you're both demonstrating a lack of empathy.

Surprising as it may seem, empathy reflects in our small actions, not just in the big things. For instance, when the other person comes into the room to talk to us about something that is concerning them, do we carry on looking at our phones or laptop, or watching the TV? Giving someone our full attention is so important, whether our partner or our children, and even in the workplace. The seemingly small action of looking up and acknowledging someone makes all the difference to the connection between you, and consequently shows you have empathy for them.

Beware of saying things like, 'Well, it's not really that big of a deal, is it?' or 'Oh, you're probably just overreacting.' Phrases like these mean we come across as indifferent and uncaring; but worse, it can make a person feel dismissed and alone – and disconnected from us. Long-term behaviour like this causes resentment, and a relationship will begin to deteriorate.

Giving your partner attention when he or she needs it goes a long way towards developing empathy. A simple statement like, 'I'm so sorry you have to go through this' speaks volumes, and is certainly the kind of behaviour we need to develop if we want to make our relationships work.

Make People Feel Good

"They may forget what you said, but they will never forget how you made them feel."
– Carl W. Buechner

Making emotional connections in our relationships means developing language that expresses how we feel but, most importantly, takes into consideration how we make our partner feel when we say things.

Our feelings are influenced by a whole bunch of different stimuli. Understanding those triggers provides insight into why we often react the way we do. I am very responsive to other people's voices – the cadence, the volume, the accent, the pitch, the rise and fall, the language, the intonation – and how they say a thing shapes my impression of them in the first few seconds and minutes of meeting. *Do they care about what I'm saying? Are they even listening?*

But the reverse is true, too: *Do I really care about what a person is saying? Am I really listening?*

It could be said that the use of emojis in our endless digital conversations has trivialised our emotional responses to each other; a smiley or angry or bemused face used instead of words. But on the other hand, perhaps we should pay more attention to them, because I don't think they're going away any time soon, and they do provide insight into how we have made another person feel!

However the means, though, communicating in a

way that makes people feel good is vital if we are to maintain good relationships. Even if we need to have a difficult conversation – with our partner or child or work colleague – it can be done in a way that shows respect for their feelings, and acknowledges them.

In the ups and downs of our relationships, mastering how we speak and behave, with empathy and with no judgement, only serves to strengthen our bond with each other.

Chapter 5

Be Your Genuine Self

"Be yourself. Above all, let who you are, what you are, what you believe shine through every sentence you write, every piece you finish."

– John Jakes

"*Be yourself; be genuine*" is advice that never gets old. For some people, however, to be real and genuine in their life is a very difficult task, perhaps because they have devoted their lives to pleasing other people and behaving the way they think they want them to behave. Others are not genuine because they shape their behaviour to impress, particularly around figures of authority, or in the company of people they think they can manipulate or gain something from. This non-genuine behaviour, believe it or not, can damage our personal life and ruin our relationships.

We live in an age where being authentic or being yourself is considered a rare asset; but when you find somebody who is authentic, have you ever noticed how you are drawn to them? Simply put, to be genuine and authentic requires you to be properly in touch with your feelings, thoughts and emotions, and when you're not, that's when we suffer.

There are many things that genuine people do which have become habits for them, and enable them to live an authentic life.

Genuine People Do Not Try to Be Genuine

This is actually true. Genuine people do not try to be genuine, because the moment we try to be someone we are not, we are not being genuine.

What does being our true self actually mean? It means being willing to strip away the identity we have imposed on ourselves and expose our true authentic self to the world. Being genuine also means being willing to speak the truth and express who we really are. That is what genuine people do. They are authentic to their core. They do not try to be like someone else.

Genuine People Take Ownership

Genuine people take ownership and admit their faults. They do not fall into the dangerous trap of blaming everyone but themselves if things go wrong. Think about it for a moment. How often have we found ourselves blaming our managers, our family members, the environment we live in, and politicians and the government when we are unhappy about something? If we do that frequently, it might be an idea to reflect a bit more and see if we can solve part, or all, of the problem. That is what taking ownership means.

Genuine people are often the first to forgive and say sorry if need be. They don't feel ashamed of saying sorry, and they don't hesitate when it comes to admitting their mistakes. Many people are unable to admit they are in the wrong, but for genuine people that's not a problem. They forgive and let it go, instead of allowing the issue to affect the rest of their lives.

Genuine People Treat Everyone with Respect

One of the redeeming qualities of people who take pride in their genuineness is that they do not feel they are superior human beings who are at liberty to look down on anybody else. Instead, they choose to remain humble throughout their lives. Strip away material possessions and status, and we are just human beings – and that's what genuine people understand. We are all connected, and all need to interact in some way, so let's be genuine in our respect for each other.

Genuine People Practice What They Preach

We've all encountered people who say they're going to do something but don't do it; those who are good at talking, but so often fail to act on their words. We also meet those who find it difficult to follow through on the things they claim they believe in, like punctuality, or struggle to put into practice the things they read and quite often 'preach' about!

Genuine people who believe in authenticity practice what they preach. What they say they will do, they do without a doubt. So what is the difference? They firmly believe that when they say they will do something, they *will* do it. And if they can't keep a promise – a meeting or deadline, for example – they take ownership of it and do not resort to excuses.

Genuine People Follow Their Heart

Genuine people make decisions that are true to their intuition and their heart, and not because it sounds cool or because of external pressures. They have this ability because they understand themselves; they know how they function and they know the right decision to make. (And this is often how they are able to inspire, impact and transform the world.)

Surrounding ourselves with people who have great values, a good head on their shoulders, and are genuine to a fault is essential for moving forward in life. However, we do need to ask ourselves these questions: Are they actually the person they portray themselves to be? How do we identify the people who are truly genuine before we interact with them?

Here are a few tips that will help you to spot a genuine person

1. Condescending versus Respectful

Someone who has a genuine personality will be respectful to everyone. They will take your feelings into consideration and try to make you feel comfortable. Someone who is not genuine will only respect you if you are in power, because this is how they try to gain something out of every situation; and if they have to employ acting skills to get what they want, they don't hesitate in doing so. Conversely, if they believe they have power over you, they may act in a disrespectful and condescending manner.

If a genuine person doesn't agree with another person's

beliefs or views, he or she will be respectful about it and try and understand why that person thinks like they do. Non-genuine people believe their opinions or views are the only ones that matter, and will often try to talk over people, or openly mock them.

2. Seek No Recognition versus Needing Recognition

A genuine person will never go out of his or her way to get recognition. That's the reason why a genuine person often keeps his or her actions private. Non-genuine people love to tell everyone what they're doing, because they seek praise and admiration. They also tend to think that they are better than everyone else, and will stoop to ever-lower lows to appear in a good light. A genuine person does not need to do this.

3. Hidden versus Spotlight

Genuine people understand that spending time alone can do wonders for the mind and personal development. Thus, they have no issues with staying quiet, doing their thing, without the need for attention. Non-genuine people do the complete opposite. They crave attention and will do everything in their power to stay in the spotlight. When the spotlight is on someone or something else, they will do everything in their power to get the spotlight placed back on them.

4. Humble versus Conceited

It's great when people acknowledge your achievements, but nobody likes a big-head. Genuine people prefer to not talk about themselves, and would rather talk about other people's achievements. Non-genuine people constantly brag about their achievements – that's why you might hear them tell the same story many times!

5. In Front of You versus Behind You

When genuine individuals have something they need to say to you, they have the confidence to tell you to your face. That is because they have no hidden motive. Instead, they actually hope to resolve any issue that might have surfaced between you in a rational and non-threatening way. Some people find it very difficult to do this; but there are assertiveness training courses you can go on if you want to become more confident.

Non-genuine people avoid this. They would rather talk behind your back. They might smile when you run into them, but the second you turn your back, you are their enemy. Also, they love gossip and enjoy creating a drama. It's also not difficult for them to lie and manipulate behind your back, and possibly even spread rumours about you. This is absolutely not the behaviour of a genuine person.

6. Imperfection versus Perfection

Genuine people know they're not perfect, and never shy away from learning new lessons wherever they go and with whomever they meet. They will even thank someone when they learn something from them. Non-genuine people go out of their way to be critical of anyone, in any situation. They constantly look for any mistakes people might make so they can draw attention to them, so as to elevate themselves. In truth, though, they only show themselves up for who they really are.

No Ulterior Motives versus Ulterior Motives

When a person with a genuine personality helps you, it's simply because they want to; they are not looking for any reward, recognition or praise. Non-genuine people, on the other hand, live by the 'I'll scratch your back if you scratch mine' principle. Such people only consider doing a favour if there is something in it for them.

The question in your mind right now might be 'How exactly are we supposed to deal with non-genuine people?' It is difficult to avoid them, because they are all around us. So here are some useful tips:

- Although contact is at times inevitable, try avoiding the company of people who you get a bad vibe from. Don't stick around to see if your assessment about that person is right or not; just trust your instincts and steer clear.
- If it's not possible for you to avoid them, then limit your engagement with them. Let them 'have the floor' but do not give them the attention they crave. These people are toxic and dangerous. You don't have to be influenced by them.
- The best way to deal with non-genuine people is to ignore them whenever you can. They are always trying to be the most popular person in the room, and constantly seek validation. I know it's frustrating to deal with them, but remember, they are the ones who are really suffering, which is sad.

- Whatever you do, don't stoop to their level. For instance, if you hear a work colleague gossiping about another person, just ignore them. Do not give them any encouragement.
- Call them out. Tell them to their face, politely, that their behaviour puts you in an awkward position and you are simply not going to tolerate it. The usual response, in this case, is that they will turn their attention on you, so be ready for some backlash!
- To sum up, people with genuine personalities elicit respect and admiration from others, without even trying. Their genuine behaviour is what inspires the world. In contrast, non-genuine personalities can't live without their ulterior motives, gossip and attention-seeking.
- We have the power to choose our own behaviour – genuine or non-genuine – and the company we keep. We should never be afraid to be the honest, caring people we are. Anything else is a charade.

Chapter 6

The Power of Behaviour

"Good behaviours will open doors that the best education cannot."

– Clarence Thomas

The power of behaviour is strong, and it can build and destroy relationships in an instant, both personal and professional. Sometimes, the rational and emotional modes of the brain fight each other, which results in a behavioural conflict where you either do things you know you shouldn't do, or you don't do the things that you know you should do.

Use Good Behaviour to Build Trust

Behaviour can convince people to trust you, or ensure that they mistrust you. It is a well-known fact that people who have a reputation for being trustworthy are highly regarded by those around them. Isn't that what every good businessperson does? And with that trust they gain the confidence of their valuable clients and customers and gain their loyalty. Such is the power of behaviour.

A relationship, whether professional or personal, without trust isn't really a relationship. So, what kind of behaviour builds trust?

One of the best books on the subject of building relationships and trust is *How to Win Friends and Influence People*, Dale Carnegie's 1936 classic, which has sold over 15 million copies worldwide. The book has stood the test of time, and includes advice which is still relevant today. Here are some of Carnegie's noteworthy behavioural tips that you can employ to build trust:

1. Show Genuine Interest in Other People

Carnegie believed you could build trust in two months by becoming genuinely interested in other people, instead of spending years trying to get people interested in you. When you meet new people, be interested in them, even if you think you have nothing in common. This is the first instance of behaving in a way that can make building trust really easy.

2. Talk About the Other Person's Interests

The road to gaining trust and building a relationship is to talk about the things the other person treasures the most. Carnegie considered this to be a skill which can be practised and improved. As you improve, you also increase your network and your ability to influence people. What Carnegie was basically saying, is that being a great conversationalist is all about being a good listener. The trick is to ask questions people will enjoy answering, and encourage them to talk about themselves and their interests. Mastering this behavioural skill will quickly help you build trust and stronger relationships.

3. The Power of Using the Other Person's Name

Carnegie also stressed the great importance of remembering and frequently using someone's name. He believed a person's name is the sweetest and most important sound in any language to that person, and never to underestimate the value of using it. So, next time you meet somebody new, make a special effort to remember their name and, of course, if you ever find yourself having to put their name in writing, be sure to use the correct spelling!

4. Criticise Constructively

Another useful piece of advice from Carnegie's book is the guidance he offered on giving criticism. There is one sure way of upsetting your friends, family and members of your team, and that is by telling them directly that they are wrong. Telling somebody this and disregarding their opinion is a direct attack on their intelligence and pride. Their immediate response will be to strike back and argue their point.

Instead, you can behave in a subtler manner and try asking a question which will encourage them to think about a different point of view and challenge their own ideas. Being able to deliver criticism in a constructive way is a real skill that, done well, leads to stronger relationships.

5. Reduce Tension

Another area where our good behaviour can be of much benefit is in dealing with tension. During feuds and arguments, good and polite behaviour can play a major role in reducing the tension of the moment. It also allows us to deal with the situation in a more rational manner, setting an example for others. It's undoubtedly true this can prevent a lot of the stress and anxiety that usually follows unpleasant and frustrating situations. It also works when dealing with annoying people who truly push you to your limits!

The following recommendations can help you to stick with your good behaviour, no matter how tense or annoying the situation. They'll also help you not to lose your temper and become aggressive.

6. Don't Raise Your Voice

The minute you raise your voice, it's over. No matter how hard you want to scream and yell and defend yourself, just take a few deep breaths and don't lose your calm. Focusing on your breathing and controlling your thoughts can get you through a situation without losing your temper. This sets an example for others to see that difficult situations can be dealt with calmly, without all the rage and fury.

7. Defend Yourself Politely and Assertively

When you're in a confrontation, there's a right way and a wrong way to defend yourself if necessary, and it does not mean yelling back or resorting to physical violence. It means embracing your dignity and respectfully explaining your viewpoint. Adopting this sort of behaviour always leads to better solutions to problems that might otherwise have only got worse. It also demonstrates to the other person that you will not retaliate, and that more often than not calms them down.

8. Think Before You Speak

There are ways of saying things and there are ways not to say things; and there are places to have conversations of a sensitive nature, and there are places not to have such conversations. The words you choose to speak and the place you pick to have a difficult conversation says a lot about your behaviour. If you choose to confront someone in front of other people, it will make them extremely defensive because they will be embarrassed. Instead, catch the person on their own at a more suitable time, and consider your words carefully.

9. Look for a Win-Win

Another big thing to avoid is thinking it's either you or the other person who can win the argument. This is completely flawed behaviour. It's all about listening to what the other person has to say, and understanding why that person is upset or disagreeing with you.

In short, the ideal behaviour during a confrontation is to listen, think, and then speak. Following that order means you're able to handle a disagreement or argument like a civilised person, which equals a win-win for your relationship with the person you are talking to.

10. Add Value

In all relationships, good behaviour can add value and also help in creating a great first impression. What does a person naturally seek in another person when starting a relationship or looking for an employee? It's good behaviour. Relationships, whether short-lived or long term, corporate or personal, rest on one very strong pillar, and that is behaviour. If we approach any relationship with aggressive, argumentative behaviour, it collapses like a house of cards.

This is true when making a new acquaintance, talking to customers, pitching a business proposal to a client, or asking someone on a date. No relationship will stand for long if we display inappropriate behaviour. Perhaps that's why the old saying, "*You don't get a second chance to make a first impression*" is still considered meaningful. If you exhibit polite and friendly behaviour, in no time you will come to realise that the world is your oyster.

Communication is everything, and refers to the transmitting *and* receiving of messages. To be receptive to someone, send them signals that what they are saying is being received and understood, and that their words are valued.

We communicate with more than just words, however, as our actions and body language can often say a whole lot more than the words coming out of our mouths. Have a look at the following list of behaviours. If we're honest, we are all guilty of them at times, and they can poison a relationship.

1. No Eye Contact

Eye contact is a prerequisite for any relationship to flourish. If you don't make eye contact with the person speaking, you are not giving them 100 percent of your attention. Be sure to hold their gaze as they speak. It shows that your senses are invested in whatever they are saying. It creates mutual respect. (Avoid staring, though, as this can be off putting! There is a balance!)

2. Frowning

Do you frown when talking to people? Look in the mirror and see what your eyebrows are doing when you talk. Surprising as it may seem, many people believe that frowning is a neutral expression. However, those on the receiving end of a frown will most likely interpret it as you being annoyed with them, or the conversation. Try to relax your facial expressions when talking to people. Such behaviour leaves a more polite impression on others and projects a friendlier image.

3. Interrupting

When you interrupt someone you are telling them that what you have to say is more important than what they need to say. And don't say things for them. Let them express themselves in their way. If you want to offer a counterpoint to the discussion, bookmark it in your brain and offer it when there is a pause.

4. Drumming Your Fingers or Tapping Your Foot

Drumming or tapping creates an audible interruption. It tells the person talking that you want them to hurry up and that you are getting impatient with them. When conversing with someone, keep your hands and feet still and in a receptive position, such as your palms facing downward on the desk or in your lap.

5. Rolling Your Eyes

When you roll your eyes while talking to someone, you tell the other person 'here we go again…' It conveys that you are getting annoyed either by the conversation or by the person you're in conversation with. Whatever the case, it's highly impolite.

6. A Rapid Exhale

This type of exhaling sounds exasperated, which is yet another sign of impatience. It gives the impression you are getting frustrated and want to quit the conversation. Instead, keep your breathing slow and even.

7. Flicking a Wrist

If you're making a 'shoo-fly' motion with your hand, you are unknowingly dismissing the speaker like an annoying insect. Basically, you are telling them, 'You annoy me. Go away.' Don't do this, it's highly insulting.

8. Showing Them the Palm

'Talking to the hand' puts a physical wall between you and the speaker. If you are in habit of doing this, you're telling them, 'Stop speaking. I've had enough of you.' Keep your arms at your sides as the other person speaks. This will help you to sit in a respectful and attentive posture.

9. Reading or Texting

If you're reading or texting surreptitiously while talking to someone and you think you're getting away with it, you're actually not. People can tell, and it's offensive. The signals you're sending with this behaviour to the other person are, 'I would rather be doing this than listening to you,' or 'I'm merely tolerating what you're saying.' Instead, stop what you're doing and give the person your undivided attention

10. Walking Out of the Room

This is the epitome of dismissal. By doing this, what you're saying is, 'I don't value what you're saying, and I would rather be somewhere else.' Instead, stay there and listen to what the other person is saying, however uncomfortable you feel. This is basic politeness and there's nothing very demanding in it. If you must leave urgently, wait for a pause, and then explain to the other person why you must leave

11. Dismissing Constructive Criticism

Dismissing someone's constructive criticism by saying, 'Well then, why don't you do it?' does not give the impression that you value their feedback. Rather, it displays your arrogant and narrow-minded behaviour. Instead, thank them for their feedback and tell them you will consider it and, if you agree on reflection, will act upon it.

We are all guilty of displaying some or all of these behaviours, and then perhaps wonder why our relationships are damaged because of them.

We need to practice the art of listening and observe our posture, our facial expressions, our breathing, and our movements. Remember that everyone wants to feel valued, and giving people the gift of being heard is a quality behaviour that can work miracles in our professional and personal lives, building trust and respect in every relationship.

Chapter 7

Taking Responsibility

"Wherever you are, be there totally. If you find you're here and it's intolerable and it makes you unhappy, you have three options: remove yourself from the situation, change it, or accept it totally. If you want to take responsibility for your life, you must choose one of those three options, and you must choose now. Then accept the consequences."

– Eckhart Tolle

One of the most powerful challenges in life is taking responsibility for exactly where we are and who we are. Whatever stage we're at, acknowledging that we have the ability to improve is a big part of this. But merely saying 'I'm sorry' to others, or to ourselves, is not enough. Instead, say, 'I can do better, and I will do better.'

When we accept full responsibility for our life, we take control of our behaviour. Blaming others takes away the control we have over our life.

"If your quality of life, in your mind, is determined by the actions of others, or a result of your past, you are a prisoner to that past, and at the mercy of other people

and their actions. When you are constantly blaming other people and circumstances for where you are in life, there's nothing you can do to fix it, because there is nothing you can do to fix them."

– Anonymous

What is Responsibility?

By taking responsibility, what we're doing is making a conscious choice of creating and then responding to what we create, as opposed to passively reacting to life as if it is just happening to us. This choice allows us to have more direction and discipline over ourselves. It's a highly empowered state that leads to success in all aspects of life.

Taking responsibility is also about claiming our power, and feeling the amazing sense of freewill to act autonomously. This state of empowerment means we are capable of facing and owning the consequences of any choice or decision we may make in life.

Quit Playing the Blame Game

We may not be aware of it, but we are playing the blame game more than we know within our social circle and with our friends, colleagues and family. The blame game involves finding a culprit as soon as something unfavourable happens. By doing this we can remove the responsibility from ourselves and pass it on to someone else.

The hardest truth to swallow is that we are guilty of doing this; but once we realise that's what we've been doing everything changes, because we can no longer carry on blaming circumstances, people or our environment for not being the way we want them to be.

What does this mean in real terms?

Is there something you really want to do in life? Start a business, launch your own retreat, write a book, run a course, maybe? Have you found yourself blaming someone, or something, for the reason that's not happening? Instead of sitting in the back seat blaming the driver for taking the wrong direction, or for not seeing the signs, we should actually get into the driving seat ourselves. Quit grumbling and complaining. Get in the front and start driving.

It's very difficult to take action in victim mode, because it's by far the easiest place to be. Passing responsibility to someone else means we don't need to take responsibility, or feel bad about ourselves, because we can put all those negative emotions onto someone else. It's an easy way out in the short term, but in the long term can be damaging.

Think of something you're unhappy about; something you wish you had, or had achieved, or wish was different, and notice who you're blaming for that. Take note of the reasons why you're thinking the way you are. Could it be that you are to blame, instead? That does not mean going down the 'I'm not good enough; I'm not talented enough; I'm not creative enough; I'm too shy, or I'm too scared' route, because you're still blaming if you do that – blaming yourself. That is *not* taking responsibility.

It is much better to start playing the responsibility game, which involves believing you are responsible for your own life and you're going to do something about it. That is quite scary sometimes, and it takes a lot of humility and courage to own the fact that only you can change your life. But it is so empowering.

"An important decision I made was to resist playing the Blame Game. The day I realised that I am in charge of how I will approach problems in my life, that things will turn out better or worse because of me and nobody else, that was the day I knew I would be a happier and healthier person. And that was the day I knew I could truly build a life that matters."

– Steve Goodier

How to Take Responsibility for Your Life

So, what's the big deal about taking responsibility for your life? The big deal is that it shifts our focus from being a victim to being in control. It puts us at cause and not at effect, meaning we are the creators of our life.

The next step is choosing how we respond to the challenges of being the creator. These are a few pointers:

1. Your Words, Actions, Thoughts and Feelings

Taking responsibility for these four things forms the structure of a whole new human experience. Your thoughts stem from your mind; how you feel is a sensation that you get in your body and it is the result of your thoughts; the words you speak come out of your mouth; the actions you take are a result of all three.

Taking control of these means nobody can make you think, feel, say or do anything you do not want to, in just the same way as you cannot control the thoughts, feelings, words and actions of the people around you. Realising this simple truth changes everything – and changes the way you behave, hopefully inspiring others to do the same.

2. Stop Blaming

We've talked about blame before, but this is perhaps the most important step when it comes to taking responsibility for your life. Stop blaming your parents, family, partner, economy, politicians or your upbringing for your life. Blaming does nothing but keep you in victim mode. It doesn't allow you to change the situation you're in.

Gradually, when you start accepting responsibility for your life and stop blaming others for it, you come out of victim mode and develop a more positive outlook. When you do, *you* can then take control of a situation and decide what needs to be done.

3. Stop Complaining and Making Excuses

Complaining is another type of blaming. When you complain, it's like you have no choices in life. Instead of complaining, treat every challenge as an opportunity to learn something. That is a gift. Don't waste it.

Similarly, making excuses is still avoiding taking responsibility. When you make excuses, you don't give yourself a chance to learn from your mistakes.

When there's zero personal accountability, there's

no chance of evolving into the better version of yourself. You'll be stuck in the same place. It's your choice how long you stay there.

"One day I realised that everything that I get out of life is exclusively a result of my actions. That is the day I became a man."
– Nav-Vii

4. Don't Take Everything Personally

Taking even the smallest disagreement as a personal attack is such a negative way to live. Remember, you don't have any control over the way other people behave. You only have control over the way *you* behave. *Give up the habit of assuming everything is about you.*

5. Value Yourself and Make Yourself Happy

If you're having trouble taking responsibility for yourself and your actions, chances are you might not value yourself enough. Why? Because people with low self-esteem don't usually take responsibility for their lives. If you're relying on praise from other people, then you're handing them the power to make you feel okay about yourself. Instead, value your own existence and start building your self-esteem yourself.

Making yourself happy is part of that, and a very liberating experience. It's not somebody else's job to make you feel happy. You are responsible for your own happiness. Keeping a gratitude diary is a great way to get started. If you hear one of your favourite tunes on the radio and it cheers you up, stick it in the diary. But don't stop there. Listen to it again, out of choice. You are immediately taking control for your own mood if you do this. This is just one example. There are hundreds of things you could do to make yourself happy. Go do them.

6. Use Your Power of Making Choices

We make choices all the time – red sweater or black sweater? tea or coffee? exercise or sofa? Come to think of it, even by not making a choice, you're making a choice. So why not make choices with a vision in mind; a vision for your life, your relationships, your health, and your business.

Making choices that move you forward in life and help you create your own life is power. Ask yourself if a particular decision is helping you achieve value and happiness or not, and then make your choice.

7. How Do You Spend Your Day?

An effective way to take responsibility for life is with your daily habits. Are you sleeping properly, eating healthily, giving yourself time, thanking yourself and those around you, avoiding toxic influences, etc?

Taking responsibility is more than just a state of mind; it's about your habits and what you do every single day, from the beginning of your day to the end.

8. Accept Your Negative Emotions

This is perhaps the most difficult thing to do because nobody wants to experience negative emotions. However, if you want to take responsibility for your life, you need to be able to accept them, because we all get them. It's about being honest with who you are.

Many spiritual gurus believe that accepting your emotions as part of who you are leads to greater maturity.

"Listen to your being. It is continuously giving you hints; it is a still, small voice. It does not shout at you. That is true. And if you are a little silent you will start feeling your way. Be the person you are. Never try to be another, and you will become mature. Maturity is accepting the responsibility of being oneself, whatsoever the cost. Risking all to be oneself; that's what maturity is all about."

– Osho

9. Do What You Say You Will Do

There is no better way to take responsibility for your life than keeping your word. It proves you are trustworthy and living a life that is defined by integrity. You lose credibility when you say you will do something and don't do it. In short, it's almost impossible to take responsibility for your life when you cannot keep your word.

Here are three simple principles to help with this:

- Never promise to do something unless you are certain you will be able to do it.
- Every time you make a commitment, put it in a diary or in your phone so that you remember it.

- If you're forced to break your commitment, don't make excuses. Own it, apologise, reschedule.

Being honest with yourself and those around you helps everyone in the long run. And you will develop a reputation for being someone people can rely on, earning you respect and boosting your self-esteem.

10. Focus on Action

This is another critical part of taking responsibility. Having goals and ambitions in your life prompts you to act, and it feels so great when you do.

Even if your action involves taking small steps, your life will feel very different. Remember, taking action starts with your habits. Soon these small steps become habits that create more action. That's just how it works.

"An idea not coupled with action will never get any bigger than the brain cell it occupied."
– Arnold Glasgow

Taking control of your life demands order and perseverance. It also requires prioritisation. Prioritising your tasks encourages that order – the required discipline that enables you to control your life. Here's a famous analogy that emphasises the importance of prioritisation:

The Original Story (source unknown)

"A professor stood before his class and had some items in front of him. When the class began, he wordlessly picked up

a very large and empty mayonnaise jar and proceeded to fill it with golf balls. He then asked the students if the jar was full. They agreed that it was.

The professor then picked up a box of pebbles and poured them into the jar. He shook the jar lightly. The pebbles rolled into the open areas between the golf balls. He then asked the students again if the jar was full. They agreed it was.

The professor next picked up a box of sand and poured it into the jar. Of course, the sand filled up the spaces between the pebbles. He asked once more if the jar was full. The students responded with a unanimous 'yes'.

The professor then produced two cans of beer from under the table and poured the entire contents into the jar, effectively filling the empty space between the sand. The students laughed.

'Now,' said the professor, as the laughter subsided, 'I want you to recognise that this jar represents your life. The golf balls are the important things – your family, your children, your health, your friends and your favourite passions – and if everything else was lost and only they remained, your life would still be full. The pebbles are the other things that matter, like your job, your house and your car. The sand is everything else – the small stuff.'

'If you put the sand into the jar first,' he continued, 'there is no room for the pebbles or the golf balls. The same goes for life. If you spend all your time and energy on the small stuff, you will never have room for the things that are important to you. Pay attention to the things that are critical

to your happiness.

'Spend time with your children. Spend time with your parents. Visit with grandparents. Take your spouse out to dinner. There will always be time to clean the house and mow the lawn. Take care of the golf balls first – the things that really matter. Set your priorities. The rest is just sand.'

One of the students raised her hand and inquired what the beer represented. The professor smiled and said, 'I'm glad you asked. The beer just shows you that no matter how full your life may seem, there's always room for a couple of beers with a friend.'"

'Filling the Jar of Life' (Borrowed and slightly adapted here, with thanks)

Lots of people talk a very good game, but we judge people not by what they say but by what they do. Since the only behaviour we control is our own, it must match the words we speak. Consider the following elements adapted from the famous analogy of the Jar of Life:

- Golf balls *represent our genes, our uniqueness and predisposition to behave in a particular way.*
- Pebbles *represent all the small things and activities that we choose to do.*
- Sand *represents all the relationships and connections that bind us together.*
- Beer *represents our lifestyle.*

This philosophical analogy provides valuable insights into prioritising our stones, pebbles, sand and beer. Taking responsibility for who we are is crucial if we want to fit all these other amazing things into our lives, and have time for a beer with friends. And it begins with the thoughts, feelings, words and actions that we choose to shape our daily habits.

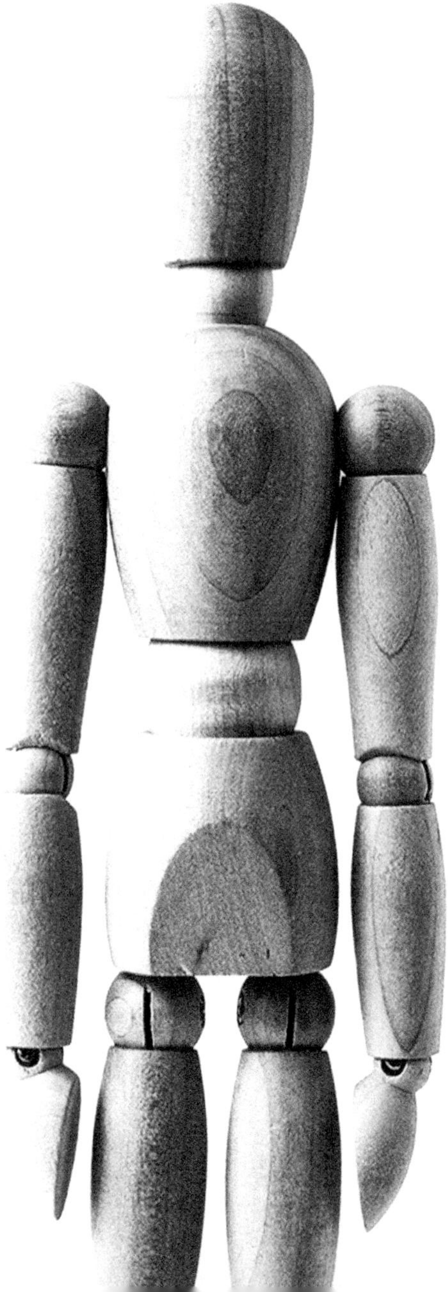

Chapter 8

Choosing Your Behaviour

"Your behaviour is a choice: it isn't who you are."
– Vanessa Diffenbaugh

Our behaviour does not have to control us, we can choose to control our behaviour. And it starts with our thoughts

Controlling Our Thoughts

We all have both positive and negative thoughts, but if we have more negative thoughts than positive, we are going to have a rather dismal life! However, if we can learn to control our thoughts, life really does open up to us in a different way.

The universal law of attraction states that "*thoughts become things*"; in other words, we attract the things that our negative or positive energy put out. Another way of looking at it, is that thoughts, which are electrical impulses, affect the events we experience in our lives, for good or for bad.

So, how can we control our thoughts when we have, on average, 60,000 to 80,000 *a day*?

One way is by replacing every negative thought that surfaces in our mind with a good thought. We can do this by looking at them as they pass through our minds, and weeding out the negative ones. It's not always easy, but well worth practising!

Let me give you a specific example. Maybe you feel resentment against someone because of something they did or said, and you feel a flash of anger every time you think about them or see them. Holding on to that feeling of resentment – which is instantly triggered the moment their name pops into your head – will keep you in a negative thought pattern, and for as long as you hang on to that negativity it will affect the way you speak and act around that person, creating more negativity. The only way to stop this loop is to literally change the way you think. So they upset you. Perhaps they were having a bad day? Perhaps you said something that pressed their buttons and made them react badly to you? Think about this, and when they next appear in your thoughts, change the thought. Replace it with something compassionate, or kind, or something that you like about that person. Keep doing it until it becomes a habit to think well of them. Next time you see them, you'll have a different experience.

A more general example could be applied to when we wake up every day. Instead of groaning and going back under the duvet with a head full of what-ifs – *What if the train is late? What if that idiot from Accounts is in the meeting?* – it would be better to lie in bed for a few moments and think *Today I'll only see the good in people* or *Good stuff always comes to me,* for example. This might sound a bit contrived, but these are the kind of vibes we need to put out more often.

According to the Buddhist monk Matthieu Ricard, *"Thoughts can be our best friends, and our worst enemies."*

Everyone has experienced a moment when their mind seems to have a mind of its own. However, when we take control of our thoughts, we feel happier, less stressed, and better equipped to solve problems or attain goals.

Our thoughts have a deep impact on our behaviour. We can become angry, frustrated, depressed, lonely, disappointed, worried, fearful, sad or doubtful because of one negative thought. On the other hand, a single pleasant thought can make us smile, laugh out loud, feel a sense of pride, cause us to relax, or make us feel more confident.

Simply put, our thoughts are directly controlling us for the majority of the time, whether we are consciously aware of it or not. That's not how it should be. We need to learn to control those thoughts in a simple yet effective way.

STEP 1: Learn to Stop Your Thoughts

We can learn to do this regardless of whether they are positive or negative, just to give ourselves some thought-free time to gather ourselves in a hectic day. This is difficult, but well worth the practice. And when it comes to negative thoughts, try pressing a figurative Stop button if they get unmanageable.

STEP 2: Identify Your Negative Thoughts

The better you become at stopping your thoughts, the faster you will become at spotting a negative thought and dismissing it if it is of no use to you. There are times though when negative thoughts do need attention, because you need to figure out what it is about that meeting or project or person that is making you feel anxious. Give yourself permission to look at this. It's interesting how quickly we can work a thing out if we do this, rather than hurtling down a long stream of anxious thoughts with no control.

STEP 3: Write Your Thoughts Down

Writing down your negative thoughts helps because it gets that thought out of your mind and on to paper. As long as it stays inside your mind, it seems more powerful than it really is. Once you have written it down, you can distance yourself from it, and the emotion it creates within you, and analyse it far more rationally.

STEP 4: Find the Lie

More often than not, negative thoughts stem from a lie about yourself that you believe to be true. It's a key step identifying that lie and facing it. The lie could be anything; for instance, 'I'm worthless,' or 'I'm a failure,' or 'I'm a loser.' Look at why you believe that. Maybe somebody told you that you're a loser and you will never achieve what you intend to in your life. Whatever the lie is that has been fed to you, write it down to get it out of your head.

STEP 5: Recognise the Truth

The only way to kill the lie that is causing all the negative thoughts is to recognise the truth about yourself. You could seek spiritual guidance, meditate, pray; or you can involve your best friend, or someone else you trust, who'll offer you an outsider's perspective. Once you have the truth you're looking for, write it next to the lie. But write it using positive phrasing. For example, instead of writing, '*I am not a failure,*' write down, '*I am a successful person who has accomplished many great things.*'

This exercise empowers you and demonstrates that you can control your thoughts – both negative and positive – and it will not only stop negative thinking, it will increase the number of positive thoughts and the associated emotions

Controlling Your Feelings

Feelings and emotions are a most pressing and sometimes painful force in life, and we are all driven by our feelings every single day. We take chances because we feel *excited* about new prospects. We yell at someone because we feel *angry*. We end up crying because we feel *hurt*. There's no denying the fact that although our thoughts trigger our feelings, our feelings dictate our thoughts, intentions and actions.

Like any other aspect of life, emotions need to be controlled, especially the negative ones. But they are the ones that must be handled with extreme care.

Negative feelings, like envy, bitterness or rage, tend to get out of control once they have been triggered. In time, these emotions can grow, gradually conditioning the mind and dominating our daily life. A person who is perpetually angry wasn't born like that; they just allowed certain emotions to continue for so long that they became habitual.

So how can we avoid operating from these negative emotions and master them, particularly when faced with difficult circumstances?

1. Do Not React Right Away

Steer clear of reacting immediately because it triggers emotions you want to avoid, which is almost guaranteed to end up in you saying or doing something you will regret. Whenever you feel like your emotions are taking over, take a deep breath and stabilise the overwhelming impulse. This will support you in calming down.

2. Seek Spiritual Help

It is said that faith can be a saving grace in the darkest of moments. Establishing a relationship with the divine world, however you see it, may well help you. That's because when you place your faith in a higher force, you also believe in the power of divine intervention to guide you and show you what you must do in trying times. So, when feeling burdened with emotion, close your eyes, and ask the universe to illuminate the best path forward.

3. Release Your Emotions in a Healthy Way

Once in control of your emotions, it's time to release them in a healthy way because all that adrenalin has to go somewhere. The best way to do that is to go to someone and share your feelings with them. Hearing an opinion other than your own makes a world of difference. It also broadens your awareness. You could also keep a diary and write your feelings in it. Some people find it helpful to engage in sports like kickboxing or martial arts.

4. See the Bigger Picture

Everything happens for a reason. So when something unfavourable happens in your life, before letting the surge of negative emotions take you over consider that maybe it's an opportunity in disguise. You may not see it in the beginning, but you may see the bigger picture eventually. For instance, a relationship break up is a hard thing to deal with, whether it was your idea to part or not. But maybe you'll get to meet your soulmate now? Or someone you really click with, who shares your interests and goals?

5. Forgive the Emotional Triggers

Sometimes an emotional trigger comes because of a close friend or a family member. You may feel a sudden rush of anger at something they said every time you see them, or, alternatively, a stab of self-loathing when you recall something you could have done differently. When you forgive, you detach yourself from that feeling, whether resentment, jealousy, anger or regret. This helps you let others be who they are instead of letting your negative emotions escalate, and acknowledges that you are not perfect.

6. Replace Your Thoughts

As we've discussed. negative emotions promote negative thoughts and vice versa. This creates a cycle of negativity. Whenever you are confronted with an emotion that makes you feel bad, replace it with a different and a more pleasant thought. Sometimes just thinking about someone who always makes you laugh, or remembering a happy event is enough to change the thought.

If we allow the negative feelings that filter through our minds and cloud our thought processes to multiply, we may make wrong decisions. In order to avoid the repercussions of acting out during an emotional upsurge, try to calm your intensified spirit and quiet your troubled mind. When the difficult moment has passed, you will be grateful you were able to master your emotions.

Controlling Your Attitude

"Attitude is more important than the past, than education, than money, than circumstances, than what people do or say. It is more important than appearance, giftedness or skill."
– Charles Swindoll

"Improve your attitude, improve your life" – that's what behavioural experts say. Yet it takes a tremendous amount of effort to build and maintain a positive mental attitude. But changing and improving our attitude can help us change the way we see and do things. Perhaps you've heard the saying that "attitude is more important than aptitude" to succeed in life? Well, there's a lot of truth in that statement.

We have all been conditioned to see and do things, even think, in a certain way. With practice, we can improve our attitude. There are several things we can do here:

1. Stay away from negative and pessimistic people. The company you keep matters a lot. If you hang out with people who are always grumbling and complaining, then you need to avoid them. Staying 'in' with them will make it normal for you to look at life and the people around you in a negative light, too. Somebody once said that we are all the average of the five people we spend most time with.

2. Do not complain and blame others for your problems, mistakes, setbacks and misfortunes. Only you are responsible for your actions and their consequences. Only you are responsible for your life and circumstances.

3. Be more in touch with your feelings and thoughts, and try not to get carried away by your worries. No matter how difficult the situation is, make a conscious decision to begin your day, every day, in an optimistic and positive way.

4. Keep a positive attitude towards the people and events in your life. You cannot always control what happens in your life; but you can control how you react to what happens. This will help you build the confidence, courage and motivation to change, improve and find better and rewarding solutions to life's ups and downs.

5. Learn to adapt. We know for a fact that things change and so do circumstances. Thus, try to adjust to what is going on around you rather than fighting it. Also, never see change as a threat, because it can be an opportunity to learn, to grow, to evolve, and to become the best version of yourself.

6. Face your reality with courage. Take a good and careful look at the situation you are in and allow yourself time to think. See where you are standing now, and decide what you want and where you want to be in the near future. It's important to realise you have the ability and the potential to change yourself and to change things.

7. Instead of comparing yourself to others, concentrate on the things that you are good at. There is nobody else like you, so believe in your capability of using your strengths – your integrity, your work ethic, or your empathy, for example – to do great things with your life.

Never stop looking for different or better ways of doing things. By allowing yourself to see beyond what others think is possible, practical or wise, you give yourself a great shot at being highly productive and achieving some really great things, personally and professionally.

A Perfect Example for Choosing Your Behaviour

You will have heard the following two phrases: "walk the walk and talk the talk," and "walk one's talk." They might appear to be the same thing, but they have opposite meanings. To "walk the walk and talk the talk" means to put up a good front, to be good at being phoney and appearing in a way that impresses people. It is about insincerity and faking your way to success. Another phrase from Hollywood – "Sincerity is the key to success in Hollywood. Once you can fake that, you can get anything" – is another way of saying the same thing.

In contrast, "to walk one's talk" is to live with integrity. Whatever our own "talk" is – whatever we believe and say – we *do* what we say.

The following classic story of Mahatma Gandhi illustrates this:

"When Gandhi was older, he was famous all over India. People would line up for hours just to ask his blessing or to ask him one question. He always gave a wise, polite and encouraging answer.

One time, a mother brought her child. She had waited for hours. She asked Gandhi to tell her child to stop eating sweets because they were ruining his teeth. Gandhi asked her to come back in two weeks, and he would do it. Everyone was shocked – he had never done anything like that before.

Two weeks later, the mother came back and Gandhi wagged his finger and said to the little boy, 'Stop eating sweets! They ruin your teeth.' The woman thanked him and then said, 'If I may ask, my dear Gandhi, why didn't you just say this two weeks ago?'

Gandhi smiled and answered, 'Two weeks ago, I was still eating sweets!'"

That's what it means to walk one's talk!

The world is full of people who have set an example by managing their thoughts, feelings and attitudes, and whose behaviour is a manifestation of that. Do not think this is something that only happens for other people. Or that what happens to you and who you are is simply your destiny. It is not! Thinking this way sends a message to our brains to stop looking for new ideas and better ways of doing things. It is never too late to change this programming and get on the way to being a better, more controlled version of ourselves. And we might just surprise ourselves along the way!

Chapter 9

Don't Let Others Define You

"Don't let others define you. What you think of yourself is what really matters the most."

– Anonymous

We live in a world where everybody seems to have an opinion on how we should live. One of the main things we need to instil in ourselves is to not let anyone – our friends, families or partners – define us. It's imperative that we be the only judge of what we should do and how we should live our lives.

This won't stop the people we spend time with thinking they can judge what we do anyway. Some seem to think they have some kind of license to criticise others; and what's worse is that the people who are afraid of being judged are often the ones criticised most.

So what should be our response to people who are determined to criticise or define us?

Avoiding the company of such people would be the best idea; but if you can't avoid them, don't take whatever they say personally. A huge amount of freedom comes to you when you do this. You need to learn to evaluate yourself independently of how others evaluate you. Let's look at what that means in more detail.

What Does This Mean?

What this means, in essence, is that you need to do what you need to do, and be who you need to be. There are many things that shape you as an individual – gender, race, age, religion – and society has created a thousand different labels for every aspect of our lives. It's very easy to absorb them, and think that's who you are, and only who you are. And with the way social media works, people are far too quick to judge and criticise others based on these labels.

Is it possible that you have fallen victim to letting others – whether it's somebody you know individually or society – define you by judging what you should be doing rather than doing what you want to do? How does that make you feel?

It's important that you are this honest with yourself, because the steps you want to take won't get taken if you don't. You might need to shake a few things up in your life, but if it means honouring who you want to be, do it. For instance, what if you've always been told, 'Oh, nobody in this family goes to university,' but your absolute passion is to study law, or languages, or whatever it may be? Are you going to let that stop you?

You need to be the author of your own destiny. It doesn't really matter what has happened in the past, you have to focus on the present and change your life because you want to, and because you can.

Why You Should Not Let Others Define You

Surprisingly, it's often the people who care about you the most who try to define you, and maybe out of good intentions, because they don't want to see you struggle. However, they are taking control of your happiness and chance to do something you really want to do when they do this. You have a combination of unique talents and curiosities. Use those to figure out who you want to be. When you let other people define you, you give those talents and curiosities up – to them.

So, you might struggle. You might feel like giving up sometimes. You might not even know how to get started. But every single step is a vital lesson in learning about who you are, and you will feel so fulfilled when you make it. A friend of mine was taught to believe that further education was a waste of time. She's now studying for an honours degree, in her fifties, and loves every second despite how hard it is sometimes. She is alive with passion. You can see it in her eyes and hear it in her voice.

When you watch a movie, you choose the movie that you want to watch, because it interests you. Shouldn't it be like that with your life? Shouldn't you choose the things you want to learn? Because if you choose to do these things, you are going to enjoy every single second that much more.

Don't Let the Opinions of Others Hold You Back

It is human nature to want to be liked, loved and accepted. However, if you worry too much about the opinion of others, you run a real risk of being held hostage, and fear will never let you become the person you want to be.

The 21st century is like no other time in history. Social media has taken over our lives. Our life is now public. Everybody knows our business (if we choose to post about it, that is!) and therefore everybody, unfortunately, has an opinion on it. It's now harder than ever to break away from the crowd, without the crowd questioning or criticising our decision to do whatever we choose to do.

Consider these three reasons why you cannot let fear of the opinion of others influence your decisions.

1. Time is Limited

Our life is a ticking clock. Every second that passes away is not going to come back. Also, we're not getting any younger! As uncomfortable as that might sound, truly embrace this fact and stop being precious about things that don't matter and get started on the things that do – the things that make you, you.

2. Regret

A famous Australian nurse once interviewed people as they laid on their deathbed, and she found that the single most common regret of the dying was wishing that they'd had the courage to live a life true to themselves and not the life that others expected of them. That's because when people look back on their life, they have a retrospective clarity that only exists in those precious hours and minutes; everything pales into insignificance, and only that which truly mattered is considered.

Nobody has the right to tell you what's best for you,

or the right to force you to live a life that isn't true to your ambitions and wishes. So, make your own decisions, and have the courage to tackle each obstacle along the way. But most of all, enjoy it!

3. People-pleasing is Impossible

People-pleasing is impossible because it's impossible to live up to everyone's expectations. The other point here is that in doing so, you fail to please the most important person of all: yourself. The harsh reality is, people don't always care about you as much as they say they do; it's more about wanting to control you for their own gratification. There's the famous quote that says, "*We would worry less about what other people think of us, if we've realised how rarely they do.*"

It's time to stop living life bowing to other people's opinions. Find your own happiness and discover who you truly are.

How to Not Let Others Define You

At times you may feel disheartened because you're carrying around the words and judgements you have heard at different points in your life. It may even feel as if those words and judgements made by others were written into the code of your DNA.

Sometimes it just so happens that you allow people to take from who you are, and make you who you have come to be, because you had no choice at the time. Perhaps you had a very domineering parent, or your religion or culture dictated your behaviour and choices? And sometimes we are our own worst enemy, because we can see we are being controlled and take the easy option because anything else is going to rock the boat.

The words people say and the things we are taught, they can have a huge impact on us.

Think about this deeply. Have you ever let criticism or judgements from your past hinder who you are in the present? Have you allowed those words to impact what you are truly capable of doing? If yes, now is the time to take back that power. Let's look now at a few ways of doing this.

1. Bring the Troubled Feelings to the Surface

It might take time, but dig deep enough to bring up some of the deep-rooted views you've accumulated over the years. Those views include other people's words and judgements about you, which have followed you wherever you go.

If you don't do this, you'll continue to relinquish control of your life and remain on the same path. Acknowledge that those words were only someone else's opinion and can no longer affect you or harm you. Those words stopped you from becoming who you were meant to be. Not anymore. Root them out. You don't need them.

2. Share Your Feelings with Someone Close

There are many instances in life when we feel shame about the criticisms and judgements we have faced and how they affected us, so we keep those criticisms to ourselves. We tend to think those words have already done enough damage, so why expose such raw feelings?

However, keeping those feelings inside is letting them define you. Saying how you feel, out loud, to someone who genuinely cares about your wellbeing and supports you, is incredibly liberating. Just as writing things down can help, so can bringing out the feelings you have kept hidden for so long. Sharing those feelings with another person, who can be there for you and serve as a support system, really does cleanse your mind and body.

3. Surround Yourself with Positive People

Sometimes we don't have a choice, and have to be around negative people, but keeping the company of positive people as much as we can is an amazing tonic. It's hard to find people who have your best interests at heart sometimes, especially if you've been used to hanging around with a certain group, but keep looking. Go to places you wouldn't normally visit. Get brave and talk to people. Positive people will not attempt to bring you down. They will truly care about you.

It's not easy to let go of people you have already formed relationships with, and maybe they've been around your whole life; but if they continue to impose their negative attitudes on you, they'll just carry on bringing you down to their level, which is counterproductive to your decision to take back control.

4. Keep Reminding Yourself Who You Are

It's easier than you think to get caught up in what others say about you; and it doesn't take long before you begin to see yourself in that light again. Don't lose sight of who you truly are, and the unique qualities you have within yourself.

Take the time to look at who you are, and who you will still become, on your terms, *not theirs*. You are your own person and must choose not to be moulded by other people's opinions any longer.

Further to this, remember that people can only take from you what you allow them to take – and that includes your freedom of choice. If you allow others to define who you are, you are giving them the power to dictate where your path will lead and handing all the choices to them. It's time for you to decide; it's time for you to define who you are.

Chapter 10

Be Expressive

"Life is very, very short, and you can choose to live it how you want. You can choose to dumb yourself down and not express yourself just so you can fit in, just so people won't dislike you."

– Gerard Way

A life spent not expressing who we are, what we stand for, what we believe in, what our values are, and, above all, how life makes us feel, is a sad way to live.

Being expressive is a good and healthy behaviour, but how do we do that without appearing opinionated, arrogant and full of ourselves?

There are many important factors to expressing our beliefs, opinions, needs and feelings. Let's look at some of those, and then we'll discuss how to express ourselves without scaring people away, boring them, annoying them, or making them fear asking us for our thoughts on a subject

The Need to Express Yourself

Sometimes our emotions are so strong we want to laugh or cry or scream. As obvious as it might sound, it's healthy to just let those feelings out; and there's plenty of evidence that expressing yourself is good for you, both physically and mentally. (But there is a way of doing it, which we will go on to discuss!)

For example, in a study of 111 people in 2013, researchers found a small, positive correlation between a person's score on an emotional suppression scale and their mortality risk – basically how likely they were to die for any reason. It's not clear exactly how suppressing emotions might lead to our death, but it could be that it makes it more likely that we will choose 'unhealthy' outlets for our feelings instead, like smoking or drinking, or unnecessary risk-taking.

Other research has linked how handling being angry and hurt with aggressive behaviour is also not great for our overall wellbeing. Doing this also shows a lack of regard for the wellbeing of other people. And interestingly, those who try to suppress their angry feelings can often end up being even more aggressive when they do 'blow', which is, again, showing a lack of respect for the person on the receiving end.

Other studies have connected emotional repression on the one hand, and explosive expression on the other, to greater levels of stress and anxiety.

So, keeping our thoughts, feelings, desires and beliefs to ourselves is clearly not an option; but then neither is expressing them in a way that damages our health. Expressing ourselves in the right way is a great discipline, and shows others we are in control of our emotions and behaviour – which is better for all concerned.

Prerequisites for Authentic Expression

Expression is authentic when it emanates from your heart; but you don't have to raise your voice to let others know what you think and how you feel. The ability to truly express yourself will come if you develop a sense of being secure in yourself, knowing who you are, and what you stand for.

However, the problem is that not everyone can express themselves, and this can be for several reasons. Maybe they do not know who they truly are. Maybe they've been shouted down, too many times, and are afraid to express themselves. Maybe they've never been shown how to share their thoughts effectively. As a result, they keep their ideas, thoughts and feelings to themselves.

So, what's the solution?

You need to discover yourself, work out what your beliefs and values are, and take the courage of those convictions in both hands and share them with those who will listen, and who care about how you feel. Once you do that, self-expression has the power to transform your life, because you can finally live in alignment with who you are, and authentically express it to the world.

However, there is one thing you need to be careful about: self-expression requires a safe environment. Therefore, make sure that the person, or people, you talk to really do have your interests at heart, and won't diminish you by mocking you or shouting you down. We talked about finding the right kind of people in the previous chapter, and they are out there. The last thing you want is to invite hurt and humiliation by expressing yourself in the wrong circles.

There are many prerequisites for expressing yourself. We'll look at some of them now.

1. Thick Skin

This means having a certain amount of resilience, because when you share your ideas and values, not everyone is going to agree with you. You need to be ready for the response. You need to be ready for the feedback. Because that's what positive people do for each other: they listen, they respond. Whatever that response is, you shouldn't take it as a personal attack. It's part of the process of learning to express yourself and accept the feedback.

2. An Open Mind

This works both ways. Keeping an open mind means we don't fight who we are becoming; we embrace all the emerging thoughts and feelings and views. It also means keeping an open mind to maybe taking a slightly different direction with those views if we need to. For instance, we mentioned the desire to go to university. Sharing this thought in trusted company is a major step in making that happen. But what if it's suggested that maybe we should choose a more vocational subject, or something completely different to what we imagined ourselves studying? Accepting the fact that perhaps these trusted people have a point is all part of keeping an open mind.

3. Courage

Again, there are two parts to this. The first is having the courage to listen to your own self emerging, and avoiding the sort of company that will show little respect for who you want to become. The second is finding your voice and sharing this new you. But there is no greater way to learn than to step into the ring and start talking. Every time you do, your courage will grow.

4. Believe in You

You have to believe in yourself to take the stand and express your thoughts, beliefs and feelings. If you don't believe in yourself, it's highly likely you might bottle it and hold back.

5. Acceptance

This is similar to the previous point. You have to accept yourself first before anyone else can. When you do, you will speak with conviction and authenticity.

6. Be Yourself

This is perhaps the most important prerequisite for expressing yourself. This shows you have a grasp on all of the above; you are sure of what you believe you can become, and now have the courage to share yourself. Just be you, and let the cards fall where they may.

How to Present Who You Are to Great Effect

It is never okay to dismiss or violate the beliefs and values and feelings of other people. And it is never okay to present your newfound knowledge about yourself in an arrogant way. This will undo all of the hard work put in to get to this point. So how should we present who we are, and in a way where we attract respect and support?

- Know Yourself First

You need to know who you truly are, at your core, when it comes to expressing yourself. Without knowing yourself, how can you talk about what path you'd like to take, what actions you'd like to carry out, and decisions you wish to make? Truly knowing yourself will mean you can express yourself clearly and honestly.

- Know What You Are About

Similarly, be really clear about what you represent, what you stand for, what your values are, and why. Once you have definite answers for all these questions, you will be able to express your ideas, your point of view and your feelings in a powerful way.

- Find the Best Form of Expression

The expression of your inner voice should sound like it's *you* talking. Ask yourself if your expressions feel right, and feel like you – and not a 'borrowed' persona from YouTube! Keep your audience in mind, too, and be just the right amount of passionate or calm to suit who you have chosen to talk to.

- Listen to Your Intuition

Your intuition is a sense of inner knowing and inner awareness. Use it. It will tell you the suitable ways in which to express yourself. If you think singing, dancing, jumping, joking, making a meme, or whatever it may be, will help you express your ideas, thoughts and feelings, then go ahead and do it.

- Dress Intuitively

The way you dress says a lot about your inner self; that's why the clothes you choose are a great way to express yourself. Therefore, wear clothes that suit your style, mood and personality. Dressing the part will also help you stand out, and adds to the message that says you are confident and happy about who you are becoming.

- Leave a Lasting Impression

This, so often, can be about so much more than what you need to say. It can be about your smile, your laugh, the way you make eye contact or engage with who you are talking to. And it all proves you are becoming the master of your behaviour, and care about the impression you are making.

- Focus on Your Body Language

Your body language has to match your voice, otherwise what you need to say will lose its impact and authenticity. Your body language should be confident but not aggressive.

- It's Not About Seeking Approval

Be confident and express your heart out. This is difficult when being yourself has attracted criticism and mockery in the past. This new you, it doesn't need outright approval, it just needs to be heard.

- Use Positive Affirmations

Using positive affirmations is a great way to remind yourself of everything you need to express yourself. Say, 'I have the courage to express myself fully; I know who I am; I believe in myself; I'm okay with sharing who I am with others.' You will be amazed by the power of the spoken word mixed with self-belief.

- Increase Interaction With Confident People

Being around people who are really good at expressing themselves will give you the much-deserved inspiration to express your thoughts and opinions. Watch how they interact and engage with people, and see what sort of reaction they get.

Start practising. Talk to others, smile, make eye contact, and be present. Try sharing a piece of yourself, and gauge the response. Really *listen* to the response. All this will help you learn to express yourself in a confident, open and authentic way.

Express Yourself Often, but in a Small Way

Begin with small social experiments, and see how it feels to express your feelings and thoughts. It's not necessary to talk about something complicated or complex. Start with small ideas, and note the response. This will help you to shape the delivery of your thoughts.

Post on Social Media

Social media is an excellent platform to begin expressing yourself, and there are ample opportunities to express yourself via apps, blogs and forums. Steer well clear of negative discussions, however, as these will be counterproductive.

Ask Questions

Chances are, if you're thinking about something, others may be thinking about it as well – whether a news item or a local event. If you're unsure how to begin talking about how you feel, ask questions instead. This will get the conversation started, and then you can test how it feels to express your thoughts.

Assertive versus Aggressive Self-expression

Being assertive is not the same as being aggressive. There is a very vital distinction. Aggression is self-enhancing behaviour at the expense of others. Being assertive is the ability to express yourself without violating the rights of other people.

The whole lesson here is to develop behaviour that works in service of self-expression rather than against it. Ultimately, it means learning to express ourselves in a way that sets an example for others, and respects them, whilst sharing our deepest thoughts and feelings. There is no better way of communicating.

Chapter 11

Words Matter

"People may hear your words,
but they feel your behaviour."
– John C. Maxwell

The words that come from your mouth are like arrows shot from a bow: neither can ever come back. Words can make relationships and break them; words can create problems and solve them; words can make good things look bad and bad things look good; and words can create and remove our differences. Words, either written or verbal, have started the greatest wars in the world. This shows how powerful words can be.

The only behaviour we can control is our own, and this includes every single word we say, so it's up to us to develop a habit of words that are appropriate and considered. Nothing more, nothing less.

Why Words Matter

Some people are careless with their language. They seem not to understand that words can improve our energy, make us more creative, and enable us to do incredible things as much as they can make us feel dull and depressed, feel uncertain and insecure, or take away our energy and spirit. We therefore have a choice, every day, at work and at home, and even when in contact with strangers. We can either use words that build up, or words that tear down.

If we consider the great dictators, and how their words of hatred caused the people around them to commit abhorrent acts, we will understand the power words have to tear down. But if we look at the wise words spoken by people like Nelson Mandela, Martin Luther King Jr., Gandhi or Mother Teresa, words that inspired hundreds of thousands of people to rise above themselves and do great things in the world, we will see the power to build up.

Words certainly convince others to change their perspective on things, for good and for bad.

"We don't see the world as it is, we see it as we are."

– Anaïs Nin

Those simple words provide game-changing insight into how what comes out of our mouths is representative of who we are on the inside.

From the moment we were born we have been exposed to words – from our parents, our teachers, our play mates – and these words have shaped our 'inside' world, directly affecting how we translate our 'outside' world. And if the words we were exposed to were loaded with negativity and prejudice, is it any wonder that's how we 'see' the world? But if we want to get to a point where those programmed words no longer frame our behaviour, we need to change the words. This is a *very* powerful thing to do, and changes our entire world view.

Using Words to Change Our Inside and Outside World

If you don't believe this, simply try complimenting people rather than criticising them. When you get to work, try saying, 'That's a great shirt' or 'Good job', and watch how your words change the other person's mood.

In a deeper way, if you've only ever heard someone use derogatory language about certain cultures or races, you tend to grow up believing that is true, and your view of them becomes prejudiced, which affects how you speak and behave. If you notice this in yourself, do some research. Learn about that culture. Store new words about it and use them. Notice how that feels, and the reaction. The difference is remarkable, on the inside and the outside.

Words to Avoid

Learning to be selective with our words is a real skill, and can shift the energy we project and attract from negative to positive. Of course there will be times when we need to share a problem, or need picking up if we're low; but for the most part, try keeping your conversations positive. For instance:

- Talk about what you love to do, not what you hate doing.
- Talk about opportunities rather than obstacles.
- Talk about what makes you feel inspired, not tired.
- Talk about what makes your heart glad, not how it got broken.
- Talk about what makes you happy, not miserable.

- Talk about the things in your life that you are thankful for, not the things that are not working just at this time.
- Talk about things that give you pleasure, not pain.

Here's an interesting exercise. An American journalist, Joan Didion, said, *"I don't know what I think until I write it down."* So pull out a fresh sheet of paper, or a clean page in a notebook or diary, and draw a line down the centre. Write the words and sentences you use to describe yourself as a victim in one column, and write the words that show the things you are grateful for, and your personal strengths, in the other column. This is an effective way to analyse the words you often use to describe your life: 'I'm always unlucky in love'; 'When are things going to start going my way?'; 'I hate where I live', for example. Take a look at the other column. How does it read? Perhaps you have written, 'I've had some good relationships in my life,' or 'I love it when good things come my way,' or 'It's great that I know most people in my neighbourhood.' How does it make you feel when you read those words? Be committed to using the positive language in that column from now on.

Using words that sound and feel good have a direct impact on our energy, our focus, our momentum, our confidence, and our output. Getting those words right lifts our professional life and our personal life to a whole new level.

Words as Weapons

Words can cause more damage than physical abuse to a person. Here's a story (source unknown) that explains the effect words can have:

"An old man spread rumours that his neighbour was a thief. As a result, the young man was arrested. Days later, he was proven innocent. After being released, he sued the old man for wrongly accusing him. In court, the old man told the judge, 'They were just comments. They didn't harm anyone.'

The judge, before passing sentence on the case, told the old man, 'Write all the things you said about him on a piece of paper. Cut it up into little pieces, and on the way home, throw the pieces of paper out of your car window. Tomorrow, come back to hear the sentence.'

The next day the judge told the old man, 'Before receiving the sentence, I want you to go out and gather up all the pieces of paper that you threw out of your car window yesterday.' The old man said, 'I can't do that. The wind spread them all over the place, and I won't know where to find them.'

Then the judge replied, 'In the same way, simple words and comments may destroy the honour of a person to such an extent that a person will not be able to fix it. If you can't speak well of someone, don't say anything at all.'"

Gossips are worse than thieves because they steal another person's dignity, honour and reputation, things which are so difficult to restore.

So, remember this: when our foot slips, we can always recover our balance; but when our tongue slips, we can never recover our words.

Proof That Words Hurt

In the past 50 years, scientists have begun to explore the impact of attitude and belief on the physical body and our physical surroundings.

Probably the most interesting experiment in this regard was conducted by Dr Masaru Emoto. He took some pure water and exposed it to certain positive and negative words, images, prayers and music. He then froze it and then analysed the crystals that had formed under a microscope. What he discovered was revolutionary!

He discovered that the water to which positive words were spoken formed beautiful and symmetrical crystals. On the other hand, the water to which negative words were spoken formed disfigured crystals…

Think about that. *Positive words have a physical effect on water.* It is no wonder words affect our bodies, our environment, and those around us. (Interestingly, the human body is made up of 60 percent water.)

We cannot always limit our interactions with people who direct negative words at us; but this book is not about trying to change their behaviour, it's about changing our own, and the language we use is a huge part of that.

Language is the forerunner of change, without a doubt. If we choose to change the way we speak, we have a real chance of making a difference in our social and professional circles, perhaps inspiring change in those around us. Get used to expressing your ideas, thoughts and views in language that showcases positivity. See the difference it makes, and feel the energy of your interactions change.

Chapter 12

Trust

"Trust is the most important part of a relationship, closely followed by communication. I think that if you have those two things, everything else falls into place – your affection, your emotional connection."

– Vanessa Lachey

Relationships, friendships, business collaborations, even corporate deals, they all work on trust. But how does trust develop? How can you trust people?

My mother packed parachutes during World War II. She talked with fearsome pride about the skill required and how each parachute was marked so that they could trace accountability. That made me realise we all have parachute packers in our life; and that we ourselves are also a parachute packer. That raises two questions: *Would I jump with a parachute packed by that person?* and *Would I jump with a parachute packed by me?*

How Does Trust Develop?

A friend of mine often sends me beautiful stories. One story he sent me was about a fighter pilot who was required to para jump out of his aeroplane. The pilot asked, *"Who packed my parachute?"* Why? He was trying to establish trust before jumping out of the plane because, for the pilot, that parachute was his lifesaver. Most of us are not pilots, and rarely are our situations a matter of life and death, but day-to-day situations arise where we need support – and someone we can trust.

This simple story becomes a metaphor for the support system which develops as we grow and develop and try to make sense of the world. The first taste of trust we have is with our mother. She carried us for nine months, taking care of her body and, by extension, us. When we are born that care becomes feeding, nurturing, nursing and tending to our every need. Under normal circumstances, an intense bond of trust is developed whereby a child feels safe and loved. Even when we become older, our mothers are often the first person we go to when we are hurt or troubled, so intense is that bond. And a mother will drop everything else to 'pack a parachute' for a child who needs her. This is how strong the support system is between a mother and her child, and how trust is established in our early years

Establishing Trust in Unexpected Situations

As we grow older, we must learn to extend that trust, often getting hurt along the way; but extend it we must, because we will need it, often at the most unexpected times. I have shared the following story (source unknown) many times because it is an example of just how we can find support and establish trust in the most bizarre and unexpected situations.

"When a dangerous industrial safety situation arose in a factory, the plant was evacuated. The plant

manager and a colleague decided to inspect the situation. Things were brought under control by their actions. When the manager turned to leave the danger zone, after finding things were under control, he saw four or five workers standing just behind him. He said, 'I told you to evacuate. Why did you come inside?' The reply was, 'Sir, when you were in a dangerous situation, we were just behind you to help, if needed.'"

How do you think that manager felt? People like these are the parachute packers of our lives; those who are just there behind us, just in case they're needed. How does that happen? What makes some people willing to step up and others not? Which one are we? It's humbling when a parachute packer, lurking in the background, suddenly appears, as if by magic, and often at the moment you most need them. You may well have had this happen many times in your life. And you may have also been the one stepping in to help. Trust like this is a truly amazing human virtue.

Trust in Exceptional Circumstances

There are some situations where either you need the trusted shoulder of a friend, or times when you have the opportunity to be that shoulder. I'm talking about really tough times, when someone might feel depressed, lost, or even suicidal. With their permission, I will now share something a close friend of mine told me:

"A friend of mine, a very smart professional man in a technical marketing field, who excelled in his job (and everything), and was good-looking and charismatic, came

to me. We were good friends, but did not meet regularly. He asked if we could go somewhere to talk. We went and settled near a lake.

He looked very upset and tense. He said, 'Please help me. I have an issue with my job.' The problem was that he had simply started hating his job; and going to the office, daily, was becoming more and more difficult for him. He did not have any professional issues, and he was not sure what caused this sudden change, but he said he had become so lost that on one occasion he had even thought about suicide. That was the extent of his disillusionment.

We talked for some time, and decided that he should quit that job. He did. And his life changed for the better."

I asked my friend why this man came to him. He said he was not sure. But the incredible thing is, my friend spent almost three months helping and supporting that man get back to some sort of normality. That was 30 years ago. And they've only seen each other one more time since.

Why did this man trust my friend out of all the other people he could have gone to? I believe it is because my friend is a person with great empathy; but he is also very sharp, and honest, and can judge a situation quickly, and correctly. This troubled man could see my friend was genuine in his care, and when he stepped up, that incredible trust was strengthened beyond words.

Is that a fair description of a parachute packer, do you think?

Trust in Our Modern World

We all know what it feels like when trust is broken. It's like the whole world around us shatters. And this is true of relationships, families, friendships, business deals, even politics.

Trust is the glue that holds relationships of all sorts together. As we've discussed, a child's trust in his or her mother is their first taste of this powerful bond; but conversely, a mother must one day learn to trust her child. It is with no little nervousness that we 'let go of their hand', both literally and metaphorically, and allow them to make their own small steps in the world – walking to the corner shop, or to school, or to see a friend, for instance – trusting that they will remember to cross the road safely, not to fall into bad company, and to come home at the expected time.

There is a lot of discussion about parenting in the 21st century, and a lot of books are being written about trusting your children. One such book is *How to Raise Successful People* by Esther Wojcicki. She writes of how she allows her children to go to the supermarket and choose their own food for the lunches they pack for school. This idea fundamentally challenges our instincts to protect our children. But how else will we learn to trust them and, more importantly, for them to trust themselves as they make their way in the world?

We won't go into detail here, but it goes without saying how trust in a friendship or a relationship can be shattered by gossip or betrayal or infidelity.

In businesses and large organisations, there is

much focus on creating and maintaining a culture of trust. Organisations with high levels of trust are said to foster credibility, respect and fair treatment, and there is more interaction between co-workers and managers. This is the kind of behaviour that instils a mutual and strong trust between employers and employees. Where this is the case, companies tend to perform better, and there is consistent improvement in their productivity.

I'm wondering if we should even venture into our trust in politicians! Lately, many people are becoming more and more cynical about politicians because, coming back to our point of talking the talk, wow, can they talk. The sense of frustration and hopelessness we feel when they simply fail to deliver on that talk is tangible; and it feels like a betrayal of trust of the highest order when someone in a position of power turns their back on all the promises of change.

Sadly, this level of distrust is contagious, and we can find ourselves distrusting the authorities, our politicians, even our neighbours. What can we do about this.

Trust on a Personal Level

Every time we lose someone's trust, we lose an opportunity to have a good relationship with that person. We might find people pull out of a business contract with us, or our friends drift away. In any case, once we are known as an untrustworthy person, things can begin to fall apart rather fast, and we see a noticeable gap develop between ourselves and others. They might not take our call, or answer an email, and suddenly we find we're somewhat alone.

We need to deliver what we have committed to, and live up to the promises we have made. We need to be honest and open. These are the prerequisites for becoming a trustworthy person.

Each time we fulfil our word, people trust us more, and so it grows. It's not about creating expectation, it's simply about delivering on our word. This is what trust is on a personal level, and trust is a true mark of someone in control of their behaviour.

CHAPTER 13

Generosity

"True generosity is an offering; given freely and out of pure love. No strings attached. No expectations. Time and love are the most valuable possessions you can share."
– SUZE ORMAN

What is generosity? Would you consider it an important aspect of human behaviour? And what forms does it take? Being known as a generous person means we have a reputation for kindness, or big-heartedness, and it can show up in many ways.

Becoming a More Generous Person

Like trust, generosity can transform our world; and it starts with small changes which then ripple outwards to reach others. Here's an interesting thought: *How generous we are actually starts with how blessed we feel.* What do we mean by this?

According to people who have spent time in countries like the Sudan, with people from some of this world's poorest nations, generosity truly comes not from a place of excess, but from the heart. They have witnessed those with literally next to nothing, sharing tea and the little bit of food they have with strangers. Some even bury a can of Coca-Cola in the ground for months for a special visitor.

It is true that some of those living in poverty are often the most generous we will ever encounter. We might wonder why. It has to do with gratitude, or feeling 'blessed'.

"Out of the heart's abundance, the mouth speaks."
– Matthew 12:34 (KJB)

Be Generous with Your Gratitude

Stop often to count the blessings in your life, and be generous with the gratitude you extend to others. Let people know you appreciate them for all the things they do, large and small – and this includes all whom you have contact with, from your spouse to your children, from your work colleagues to the person who serves you in the supermarket.

Be Generous with Your Words

This means using kind, positive and life-affirming language when you speak. It means using words to build up and encourage and support.

Be Generous with Your Time

Time is a finite commodity, but time spent with someone, really listening to them, is probably the greatest act of generosity. Sharing our time with others has great benefits, because it causes us to slow down and notice if we need to change our behaviour when listening.

Be Generous with Your Story

Being open and honest about your shortcomings allows others to know that you're safe to be around, so they can just be themselves. Sharing the good and hard times that you have been through in your life lets others know that they're not alone.

Be Generous with Your Possessions

People are more important than stuff. Everything you have in life is a blessing, and sharing those blessings with others is praiseworthy behaviour. You can replace the stuff you have in your life, but you cannot replace the people in your life.

Be Generous with Your Home

Opening your home to people on a regular basis, as if you're saying, 'my house is your house', shows that you value them and see them as family. Your home is your sanctuary. Let others know they are safe there too.

Be Generous with Your Money

Money must also be seen as a blessing. So, tip your waiter or your barista really generously. Pick up the tab at dinner or buy a round of drinks. Sponsor a child. Pay someone's rent if you can, or a car payment during a tough time. Maybe even consider adding 'generosity' as an item in your monthly budget; that way you can look for ways each month to be financially generous with people, and make it a habit.

When we adopt generosity in these ways, it truly flows from our hearts and shows a deeper understanding of how abundantly we are blessed. Maybe take time today to actually write out the things in your life that you're grateful for. It could be a really long list. In fact, I hope it is. Then ask yourself with whom and how you would like to generously share those blessings.

Giving from the heart, with no expectation of return, is one of the most powerful ways we can demonstrate a change of behaviour. Perhaps we had a reputation for being somewhat ungenerous…? That can be changed simply by becoming generous in any way we can, and thus change the world of those we give to for the better, and our own.

Chapter 14

Make Your Own Decisions

"Trust your instincts, and make decisions on what your heart tells you. The heart will not betray you."
– David Gemmell

Much like not allowing others to define who we are, it is essential to remember that, as part of the development of our behaviour, we have the right to make our own decisions. Trusting ourselves to do this will have a positive impact on many aspects of our lives. It demonstrates responsibility and helps us practice accountability. But what if we don't trust ourselves because we've made poor decisions in the past? And how do we take into account all of the information and choices out there – whether to do with our career, or buying a car, or raising our children, or about our relationship – and make a decision that we are sure of?

Why Do You Need to Make Your Own Decisions?

"I've learned that while I'd be a fool not to stay open to the advice and experiences of the smart, amazing people in my life, I also need to listen to what I have to say."
– Alicia Keys

Listening to seasoned people in our life is a wise idea, but it is our heart we need to listen to because it's our life, and we should be the one who gets to decide what's in our best interests and what's not. A lot of the time people offer good advice because they've perhaps been through similar experiences, but don't let them dictate what you need and do not need to do in your life.

Having someone make decisions for you can sometimes seem like the easier option, and is a fairly common behaviour. Why? Because if we go and do something someone else told us to do and it doesn't really work out, then we can just blame them: it's their fault, because they told you what to do! But there are two things here: allowing other people to manage your life by making decisions for you; and the previous point about responsibility and accountability.

Other people making decisions on your behalf takes away your chance to manage your life, and take control of the things you wish to change. And this dovetails with learning to take responsibility for your choices, and feeling the power of personal choice.

Perhaps you have a business concept you want to bring to life, and you do some online research and come across many different ways of making that happen, and the more you read, the more confused you get. The most comfortable next step is to ask somebody if you should go ahead and do this or not. Maybe you're hoping, deep down, that this person will swoop in and make the decision for you, then, if it doesn't work out, you can point the finger at them. But where is the power in that? Where is the satisfaction of trying a thing because you wanted to, for you?

Making Your Own Decisions is Your Ultimate Power

From the moment we wake up in the morning until the moment we go to bed at night, we come across a multitude of situations where we have to make decisions. Sometimes the decisions are simple; sometimes they most certainly are not. For instance, what to study, which career path to follow, where you want to live, and who you want to be with – these are big decisions, because they will change your life, influencing both your present and the future.

So how do you listen to your heart, and why is this so important? Sure, other people's advice is often welcome, and can help to provide a broader view of your options; but, ultimately, your ability to make your own decisions is what makes you powerful and independent. *What you decide for yourself is what really matters.* It gives you direct control, and the chance to stand by your decision and own it. There is so much power in that, and it's that power that leads to more confidence and trust in yourself.

Only You Know Your Own Circumstances

Why are you the best person to make decisions that concern you? Because only you know what is really happening in your life. So, you might feel judged by other people for doing something you feel is right, which can lead them to them expressing their opinions. What can you do? The best you can do is listen carefully and thank them for their opinions, but ask them to respect the decision you have made, and that you take full ownership for the outcome.

You will never know if an option is good or not if you

never go for it; and you'll never find out what you're capable of if you're afraid of taking the first step. Sometimes there is no choice but to dare yourself to make your own choice, despite possible doubts and the fear of making a mistake!

The true sense of failure is to do nothing, decide nothing, and choose nothing.

"It's far better for a man to go wrong in
freedom than to go right in chains."
– Thomas H. Huxley

Making Better Decisions in Life on Your Own

There's no denying the fact that making choices on your own is a scary thing. I can hear you asking, 'What happens if I make the wrong decision?' That question, no doubt about it, can bother you every time you have to make a significant choice. But it's not beneficial to live in fear. There are ways to feel more confident when it comes to making decisions, and once you start enjoying making decisions, you won't need the approval of others.

- Be Aware of What You Want

When you're sure about what you want, it gets easier to make better choices. According to a report published in The Huffington Post, David Welch, Ph.D., a professor of political science at the University of Waterloo in Ontario said, *"People who aren't self-reflective are going to end up making bad decisions because they don't really know what they want in the first place."*

Ask yourself a few questions before making a decision: Will this affect my life in a negative way? Is this what I want for myself? Will I regret it later if I don't do this now? If you find the answers to these questions are contrary to what you're working towards, it's probably a good indication to change your decision, even if that means taking a harder route.

- Listen to Everyone, but Make Your Own Choice

Listen to other opinions respectfully, but when it comes to saying yes or no to a choice, decide what *you* think is in your best interest. With respect, the decisions pertaining to your relationships, job, or your general wellbeing, cannot be made dependant on the point of views of others, because they're not living your life. Their advice is just advice, not the ultimate do, or do not do, decision. The final decision needs to be made by you, relying on your instincts, and weighing up the effect on your life.

- Analyse Choices Logically

According to Psychology Today's Suzanne Degges-White, professor and chair of the Counselling, Adult and Higher Education department at Northern Illinois University, *"When you are confronted with some difficult decisions, it is important to be clearheaded and objective in your decision-making process."*

It really helps to write down everything that you're thinking while going through a decision-making process.

Once you transfer this internal dialogue onto paper, or onto a screen, things will seem much clearer. This will make it easier for you to make a decision.

- Make Decisions When You Are in the Right Frame of Mind

Your mood greatly affects your decision-making processes, so avoid making decisions when you're feeling hungry, angry, stressed or tired. Make sure you're relaxed and open. Slow down. Analyse the pros and cons. And avoid making rash decisions.

- Learn to Trust Yourself

We are often afraid to trust ourselves. PsychCentral's Cynthia Wall, a psychotherapist in private practice in northern California, explained in her book, *The Courage to Trust: A Guide to Building Deep and Lasting Relationships*, *"The person you need to trust first is yourself. No one can be as consistently supportive of you as you can learn to be. Being kind to yourself increases self-confidence and lessens your need for approval. Loving and caring for yourself not only increases self-trust, it also deepens your connection with others."*

Building the confidence to trust yourself is a task on its own. However, once you've worked on that, by listening to yourself and responding to how you feel, you will have more confidence in yourself, and you will feel better about making big decisions.

- Practice More, More, and More

It perhaps sounds bizarre, but practice making decisions and you will get better. Make a decision on your own, every day, about something. This could be something like your morning routine, your diet, how you plan out your day – anything that gets you into the practice of making decisions. According to Psychology Today's Abigail Brenner, M.D., a psychiatrist in private practice, *"Learning how to make good choices and wise decisions depends upon several factors: a person's developmental stage/age, having a general idea of right and wrong [...] understanding what the decision-making process entails, and practice!"*

The key is, do this without asking anyone for their opinion, and you will feel a boost in your ability to make choices for yourself. You will feel more in control. Gradually, you will notice that your decisions are not influenced by the people in your life; instead, they are a product of your own judgement.

Once you get the hang of it, you can be your own decision-maker. Now, that's one self-empowering quality!

Chapter 15

To Speak or Not to Speak

"Knowledge is knowing what to say.
Wisdom is knowing when to say it."
– Anonymous

Let's begin with a fable.

"A tortoise, who was fond of speaking and voicing his opinions, whether required or not, lived in a pond with two swans. When a dry spell came, there was no rain for weeks and weeks. The pond began to dry up. The two swans realised it was time for them to fly away and find a new pond with water. When they came to say goodbye to the tortoise, he begged them, 'Don't leave me behind! I too have nothing to eat and no water to live on. I will surely die if I am left here!' The swans replied, 'But you can't fly. How can we take you with us?'

The tortoise pleaded enough to make the swans feel sorry for him. Finally, the swans came up with a plan. They each decided to take hold of one end of a long stick. 'You must hold onto the middle of it with your mouth and never let go. You must not talk as long as we are carrying you! If you open your mouth, you'll fall to the ground,' the swans warned the tortoise. He promised not to say a word during the flight.

The swans flew into the air, carrying the tortoise on the stick between them. As they flew over the treetops, the tortoise felt like passing a comment on how high they were flying, but remembered what the swans had told him. When they flew over a small village, people looked up and shouted, 'Look at the swans carrying a tortoise! What a strange sight!' The tortoise thought of telling the people to mind their own business, but remembered the swans had warned him not to say anything out loud.

Soon, more people saw this unusual sight and cried, 'A flying tortoise! How strange!' The tortoise could stand it no longer. He opened his mouth to tell everyone to mind their own business, but as he did, he let go of the stick and fell to the ground and landed on his back. Consequently, his shell cracked into pieces.

The cracked shell of a tortoise reminds us of what might happen if we talk too much, or out of turn."

– An ancient fable

A fool is made more of a fool when their mouth is more open than their mind. Thus, an important aspect of our behaviour should be to know when we should speak and when we should keep quiet. Even if we feel like voicing an opinion, we should analyse the situation and see if this is a wise decision or not. A lack of restraint in this area can lead to several problems, just like the tortoise in the fable.

Determining When it is Fit to Speak

Meddling in other people's lives, whether it's our family, friends or colleagues, is something many of us are probably tempted to do at one point or another. This might involve making a passing remark, a pointed comment, or voicing an opinion.

Ask yourself the following questions:

- Am I getting involved in the situation for them or for me?
- Does the issue directly involve me?
- Do I have something valuable to contribute?
- What will happen if I don't say anything?
- Is getting involved going to put my relationship with this person at risk?

There are various situations in which taking that risk may seem appropriate. The use of drugs, alcohol and gambling are examples. So too when infidelity is the case; or perhaps when a friend's son or daughter has been seen engaging in dangerous behaviour. However, if your involvement is likely to hurt the person, you should think very carefully before becoming involved. Perhaps someone else would be better suited to have a difficult conversation such as this?

If you feel you are the best person, it's important that you don't just blurt out what you've got to say. Plan a time for a private discussion and base your points on care and support for the person you are talking to. Your thoughts need to be constructive and not hurtful, and always, always listen.

When you make up your mind to get involved,

do so prepared for the other person's adverse reaction. Remembering that this conversation is about them, not you, and that the reason you have gone to them is out of genuine concern and a desire to help if possible, will help. The moment it becomes about you and your opinion, resentment will arise, and your relationship with that person may be damaged.

Situations Where it is Best Not to Speak

Learning to stay quiet is just as important as learning the right time to speak. The following are the few instances in which it's best not to get involved, no matter how strong the temptation to do so is.

1. Your Involvement Will Offend

Some people are quick to take offence, so it doesn't make sense to get involved in their business and jeopardise your relationship with that person – particularly if it someone who you must have frequent dealings with, say at work. If people who are likely to get offended when you interfere in their matters say or do something you find objectionable, it is in your best interests to overlook the issue as their personal choice. This comes right back to your behaviour being the only behaviour you can control.

2. Your Comment Will Cause Hurt

In a situation where the person is very sensitive, or already going through a difficult time, try to consider the hurtful impact your thoughts might have. Wait for a better time; or in the case of a highly sensitive individual, decide whether it actually matters at all what your thoughts are.

3. It Will Trigger Your Own Defensive Behaviour

This is not wise at all. If you think you might get defensive if the person disagrees with what you have to say, don't say it at all. The situation will escalate, causing way more harm than good.

4. Your Involvement Will Cause Anger

If the other person is already stressed, or has a short fuse, absolutely do not go in with your thoughts and risk blowing your good intentions to the wind. No matter how well intended, your comments will be regarded as inflammatory, and the resultant anger will do damage to your relationship.

5. It Will Damage the Bigger Picture

There is no good reason to get involved in a situation if the result will be strained relationships, either personally or professionally. In the work place and in families there is a fine line that, once crossed, does more bad than good. If you think the conversation you want to have will damage a relationship, don't have it.

6. It Might Reinforce Bad Behaviour

Having a tantrum is a common behaviour in children and young adults. It's often their way of getting attention or manipulating a situation to tip the scales in their favour. Where your involvement will inadvertently strengthen a person's impulse for attention-seeking or gossiping, for instance, steer clear, as you'll just maximise the odds that the situation will be a cue for more bad behaviour.

"*A wise man speaks because he has something to say; fools because they have to say something.*"
– Plato

And that piece of wisdom just about summarises the decision to speak or not to speak perfectly. Showing restraint and staying quiet can sometimes be the wisest thing to do. If we must take matters in our hands, then make sure it is for the greater good, and not simply because we think we know best and cannot control the urge to interfere.

Chapter 16

Perceptions Form Opinions

"There are things known and there are things unknown, and in between are the doors of perception."
– Aldous Huxley

Have you ever noticed that when you watch a movie with your friends, how each one of you perceives the aspects of the movie differently? And think of a time when you misunderstood a message.

Recently, I saw a video in which the host narrated a short story about perceptual difference:

"A teacher asked one of her students a question: 'If I give you two mangoes and you plucked two more mangoes, then how many mangoes will you have?' 'Five,' the student replied. The teacher repeated the question, displaying the right number of fingers to teach the student. But still the student gave the same answer. Then the teacher remembered the student liked strawberries, so she said, 'If I give you two strawberries and you picked two more strawberries, then how many strawberries will you have?' 'Four,' the student replied.

In order to determine whether the student understood or not, the teacher repeated the question, this time returning to mangoes as the fruit of choice. Again the student replied five. The teacher got angry and asked, 'If two strawberries plus two strawberries equal four, then how come two mangoes and two mangoes equal five?' With an innocent face the student replied, 'I already have a mango in my bag.'"

Do you think the teacher was wrong? Or do you think the student was wrong? From the student's perspective, what he said was right. From the teacher's perspective, what she taught was also right. They were simply different views and different analyses for the same thing.

This proves we perceive things differently. The student was being logical in his answer; the teacher was being theoretical. Let's take a moment to try and understand why we perceive things in different ways.

Understanding What Forms Perception

We tend to focus our attention on what interests us, what is familiar to us, or what we consider important. For instance, maybe you like music from the 1980s? Or perhaps you prefer the 1960s? Or maybe you don't like music that dates before 2000. Your taste in music (and everything else) involves your five senses, and what you choose to experience is heavily influenced by the environment you live in; and your habits, values and outlook on life are all influenced by where you come from and who you associate with. Your psychological state also influences your perception, such as what you read and listen to, and why you do so.

All of these factors play a significant role in how

we perceive the world – and we perceive all experiences through these filters, and even form expectations of what will happen in the future based on them. It is these perceptual differences that influence everything: our brand preferences, our choice of transportation, and our self-expression through our haircut, clothing or jewellery. All these external symbols represent in one way or another how we view ourselves within our community and the world, and tells that 'story' to anyone we come into contact with.

Can Our Perception Be Wrong?

When two humans experience the same thing, one might have a positive response to it, while the other might have a negative response. This means nothing in this world is free from individual interpretation, because our perceptions are influenced by our individual differences and preconceived notions. So much so that even certain words can mean different things to different people. To one person, the word 'freedom' might mean freedom to imprison; but to another, the same word might mean freedom from being imprisoned. Similarly, the word 'fun' might mean jumping out of planes to one person; while another person might interpret the meaning of 'fun' completely differently, based on his perception of what fun is.

Does this mean our perceptions can be wrong at times? The answer is yes.

I once saw a disc rotating at a high speed. I thought it was a disc based on my perception that it was circular. However, when it stopped, I saw it was a square. So, what's the lesson in this example? The lesson is that when looking at things or thinking about them, don't leave out as yet unidentified factors from our consideration. Here, the irrelevant factor I ignored was the rotational motion of the square, making it appear as a disc.

When applied to our behaviour, the same is true. What we perceive to be 'circular', or true, and what is actually true are not always the same. And when we come face-to-face with ourselves, and who we perceive we are, we might wonder how we ever thought a certain action or behaviour was okay in the first place. And when it comes to our perceptions of others, we must never judge a person based only on one perspective – generally our own – and must look instead at many other factors.

But what about when we think we are right and decide to take action based on that perception? When we base our decisions on a single perception, that may very well be incorrect, and could have a profound effect on other people's lives.

"A male gym teacher was arrested for sexually harassing a young female student. The student said he led her into an equipment room and tried to force himself on her on top of some tumbling mats.

Later, it turned out that the student was lying. All of her details about the incident turned out to be false, and it was found that she made the whole thing up. However, the gym teacher lost his job, his reputation became tarnished, and his family went through hell because of this student's lies. The bigger tragedy was that all of this happened because almost everyone believed the young woman's story.

When the case was presented in court, the teacher was acquitted of all charges by a jury. Still, there were protestors who refused to believe the teacher was innocent. They believed the girl was assaulted and that the teacher was guilty. The situation remained the same, even after the girl told her Facebook friends that the whole thing was a joke and that she was playing a victim."

What this incident illustrates is that there were people whose immediate perceptions created the reality that the gym teacher was guilty. They did not see that the disc was in actual fact a square.

When we refuse to allow any flexibility in our perceptions, we close our minds to other possibilities and sometimes even the truth. A better way to live is to keep an open mind, and save our opinions or judgements until we have fully examined a situation. The key is to stay objective in our observations, keep strong emotions at bay as they can cloud our understanding, and allow ourselves to view different perspectives.

Showing Respect for Different Perspectives

As we continue to live according to what we have been taught from childhood, our mind is conditioned to such an extent that we forget our values are not universal values. This creates a wall of perception around us so strong that it is often difficult to break through it, even when we want to.

The following excerpt from *'Gandhi and the Goat's Meat'* serves as a good example.

"Gandhi had a Muslim friend who always tried to persuade him to eat meat. 'No,' Gandhi would answer him. 'Hindus don't eat meat, especially my caste. My ancestors never ate meat.' But the friend insisted: 'If you don't eat meat, you will remain weak. You have to eat meat if you want to be physically strong.'

Gandhi very much wanted to be physically strong. 'Are you sure it will make me strong?' he asked. 'Yes,' replied his Muslim friend. Since Gandhi was very weak, one evening he tried some goat's meat. That night Gandhi saw that the goat was crying inside his stomach. The goat was very miserable. Gandhi cried, 'I can't eat meat anymore! I have seen the goat crying inside of me.' And he never ate meat again."

Why do you think Gandhi hated to eat meat, while his friend loved it? It was simply the conditioning of their minds. Gandhi could not overcome the perception formed because of the conditioning of his mind, even when he wanted to, just as his friend could not understand why Gandhi did not want to eat the meat he was so used to enjoying, and which he had been told would make him strong.

Our perceptions create strong opinions that differ greatly from culture to culture, from community to community, and even from person to person. For instance:

- The values of a rich family are different to those of a poor family.
- The values of western countries are not the same as those of the east.

- The values of Christians, Muslims, Hindus and Jews are different.
- The values of a teetotaller are different to those of someone who enjoys drinking.

What follows is the tendency to express opinions based on things that are favourable to us, and those that are unfavourable. But developing a wider view allows for a different consciousness, and we will not be so hasty to draw conclusions or make judgements based on our perceptions alone. Being objective in our observations, without a doubt, is a behaviour trait that serves us well in our interactions.

Chapter 17

Let Them Speak

"Listen with curiosity. Speak with honesty. Act with integrity. The greatest problem with communication is we don't listen to understand. We listen to reply. When we listen with curiosity, we don't listen with the intent to reply. We listen for what's behind the words."

– Roy T. Bennett

It's easy to underestimate the power of a listening ear. Why? Because so often we are more concerned about what we have to say.

A lot of people believe what they have to say matters the most. Ever been in the company of someone, or on the phone to them, and you get the feeling they're barely listening to what you're saying – even if you're answering a question they have specifically asked you? Often, the moment you stop talking – or sometimes before you've had a chance to finish – they're straight in with their opinion, or have teed up a completely different subject entirely. How does that make you feel?

The Importance of Listening with Curiosity

Letting others speak means listening to them, properly, with full attention. It's an old adage that the reason we have two ears and one mouth is that we are designed to listen twice as much as we speak. In order to understand the importance of listening, it would be good to look at the reason for the conversation. Is it purely to voice our opinion, or is it to learn something from this particular person and develop our relationship with them?

If our goal is to have a deeper relationship with somebody, whether personal or professional, is it better to talk or to listen? The answer is obvious: to listen. Allowing others to speak opens the way for the following:

- We gain far greater insight into how a person thinks and feels, whether our spouse, our child, our boss or a client.
- It allows an individual to develop their skills in expressing themselves, confident that they are being heard.
- It shows intelligence and good manners to listen first, then speak, without interrupting or hurrying a person along.
- We have the opportunity to learn something from every conversation where we listen properly, rather than simply impart our own knowledge on a subject.
- As Roy Bennet said, "*listen for what's behind the words*". You cannot do that if you are talking.

How Letting Others Speak Allows For Growth

No matter how smart we consider ourselves to be, we can always learn from other people. And the only way we can discover new ideas, concepts and views, is by giving other people a chance to speak up.

Perhaps we are struggling with a problem at work, or can't figure out how to work a new gadget. Asking for help, but granting the person we ask the freedom to speak, may just solve that problem, but only if we listen. Their ideas might also open a whole plethora of other solutions or opportunities, which we may not have previously considered. Listening can change our life.

When people are not allowed to share their thoughts, voice their views, or contribute their ideas, they tend to get frustrated. And this frustration often leads to conflict. Welcoming other people's ideas shows that you care about what they have to say, and value them. This goes a long way in avoiding conflict and maintaining civility.

It also helps individuals grow in confidence. This is very important for people in leadership positions, such as teachers, parents and managers. When you acknowledge a person's idea, and perhaps even implement it, you enable them to witness that idea in action. If it doesn't work out as you hoped, everyone involved has still learnt a valuable lesson from the experience as far as their personal growth is concerned. If you shut a person down, the opposite occurs, and the long-term effects can be far-reaching. For instance, if a teacher ignores a student's ideas, or listens and then rubbishes the idea, that student may shy away from sharing his or her thoughts and opinions again. Jump forward a few years into the workplace, and you might have an employee with brilliant ideas but afraid to speak up. This is how important it is to listen.

Listening to Prompt Change

There are as many opinions in this world as there are people. But there are those who speak louder than most, insistent that their way is the only way. They want everyone else to be all ears to their opinions, and are disinclined to regard others' views as important. You can find such people almost everywhere. They are in organisations, politics, schools, and even in the family.

But the sharing of ideas is one of the most powerful ways that society progresses. It's what drives change. Almost every change through history has occurred when someone communicated their belief, or put forward their idea of change, and were heard.

In a debate, for instance, about the renovation of a local building, or the merging of a company, letting others speak allows them to reveal their passion and knowledge. It throws open a variety of options; it shows what people are capable of doing collectively when they consider the options and decide on a course of action.

There is no doubt that at times sharing opinions and thoughts can lead to conflict; but without this sharing the progression of society would be limited to one man, one voice, one way. Where is the beauty of diversity and choice in that?

How to Be an Effective Listener

Being a poor listener often occurs simply because no one ever taught us how to listen, and no one ever listened to us. So we come to a conversation greedy to speak rather than listen; hungry to meet others, but reluctant to hear them. As a result, relationships can degenerate into a socialised egoism.

Like most things, changing anything about ourselves comes down to educating ourselves. Our civilization is full of great books on how to speak: Cicero's *Orator* and Aristotle's *Rhetoric* were two of the greatest books in the ancient world. It seems no one has written a book simply called *Listener.* So let's get to how to be an effective listener.

1. Urge People On

As a great listener we need to encourage people to elaborate, to go into greater detail, to give us a little bit more. How do we do this? Try saying, 'Go on', or ask things like, 'Why did that particularly bother you?' or 'Why was that such a big thing for you?' in order to build a deeper level of engagement.

2. Ask for Clarification

Simply saying that something is lovely, or terrible, or nice, or annoying, is not good enough as a good listener. We need to ask questions that seek clarification, for both listener and speaker. For instance, if someone says, 'I'm fed up with my job,' or 'My partner and I are having a lot of rows,' we could help them focus on what it is about the job they do not like specifically, or how the rows are affecting them personally, instead of either offering a platitude or launching straight into our personal experiences and lecturing them.

3. Separate Disagreement from Criticism

There is one sure fire way to shut a person down and that is to criticise them, making them out to be wrong and ourselves right when they are trying to express themselves. This is insulting behaviour and is totally different to listening and sharing an alternative view. We may completely disagree with an idea or viewpoint, but voicing that in a critical manner will prompt hostility – not the result we are looking for as good listeners. A better way is to invite a discussion on the disagreement, where the end goal is always to improve the understanding of and relationship with that individual.

When we are in the company of people who listen well, we experience a very powerful pleasure; it is up to us to reciprocate that pleasure by staying quiet and listening. By learning to do this we cultivate an atmosphere of respect in all of our interactions, personal and professional, and put out the message that the 'listen first, speak second' way of communicating builds trust and confidence in each other, and builds stronger, more open societies.

CHAPTER 18

Love Unconditionally

"Unconditional love really exists in each of us. It is part of our deep inner being. It is not so much an active emotion as a state of being. It's not 'I love you' for this or that reason, not 'I love you if you love me.' It is love for no reason, love without an object."

– RAM DASS

Let's start with an abridged version of a story (source unknown) that puts forward an example of loving someone unconditionally.

"A mother only had one eye. Her son hated her and thought she was an embarrassment. The mother went to the field day at her son's junior school and, to her great sadness, she found he was mortified by her presence. The next day, the kids at school teased the boy, saying, 'Your mom only has one eye!' The boy went home and said, 'Mom, why don't you have the other eye? You're only going to make me a laughingstock. Why don't you just die?' The mother didn't reply.

The boy then went abroad for his studies and got settled there. He did not return home to visit his mother. One day, however, he received a letter regarding a school reunion and decided to attend the event. It was then that he visited his childhood home, out of curiosity. His mother was ill, and had a piece of paper in her hand...it was a letter to her son. The letter said:

My son,

I think my life has been long enough now. I won't try to visit you anymore, but it would be so lovely if you wanted to come visit me once in a while. I was so glad when I heard you were coming for the reunion, but I decided not to go to the school...for you. I'm sorry that I am an embarrassment to you.

My son, when you were very little, you lost your eye in an accident. I couldn't stand watching you grow up with only one eye, so I gave you mine. I am so proud of you, seeing the whole world for me, in my place.

I was never upset at you for anything you did. The couple of times that you were angry with me, I thought, 'It's because he loves me.' I love you. You mean the world to me.

The boy's world shattered at that very moment. He hated the person he had been all of his life. He hated himself for existing only for himself. The boy cried for his mother and didn't know of any way that would make up for his actions."

Unconditional love is about caring and appreciating someone for who he or she truly is. It means loving someone in spite of his or her mistakes and imperfections. We all need that. And when we look into our mother's eyes, that's when we see the purest version of love on this earth. It's up to us to extend that love when we go out into the world.

Defining Unconditional Love

Throughout the ages, poets, musicians, philosophers and psychologists have dedicated their lives to writing about and understanding love. Perhaps even deeper is the concept of unconditional love, which according to some people is the only true kind of love. Others say, however, that there is no such thing as unconditional love.

The ancient Greeks defined four variations of love. Of the four, agape is the one that closely equates to unconditional love. For those who don't know, agape love is actually a decision, a choice made to love irrespective of disappointments and circumstances. Thus, unconditional love refers to loving another person in their essence, as they are, regardless of what they do or fail to do.

"Unconditional Love is not the case of being blinded by love, but rather the resolution that nothing is more important than love."

– Talidari

We might experience being 'blinded' by love when we have newly fallen in love, as this is when we are most likely to ignore a person's faults. This kind of love is often considered unstable, because in order to love someone without any conditions, we need to be aware of both the good and bad elements of their personality. Therefore, the most important concept around unconditional love is realising that loving another unconditionally is not being blinded by love itself. Only we can decide if we are capable of such love.

Can Romantic Love be Unconditional?

Some say no. They reason that because a relationship, or partnership, is based on actions, feelings and expectations, romantic love has to function conditionally. They believe we could never love our husband or wife in the same unconditional manner as we love our child.

Others say yes; we can learn to love our partner in the true agape sense, accepting every detail of them, and not inflicting 'conditions' on the relationship. Yet relationships are conditional, and there are certain 'deal-breakers', like dishonesty or infidelity. Let's have a look at these points in more detail.

Giving Unconditional Love

"The only way love can last a lifetime is if it is unconditional."
– STEPHEN KENDRICK

The ability to truly love one another seems to be a problem in our demanding, intolerant, throwaway world. More and more of us crave for love, but are not prepared to give and, in some cases, even receive it.

Yet to love someone under any circumstance is a true test of unconditional loving, and is probably one of the toughest attributes to possess. We have too many expectations and no patience. So how can we develop the capacity to love others completely?

1. Love Yourself Unconditionally

The one place you can hone your ability to love unconditionally is with you. Start by loving yourself unconditionally first. You know your flaws, deficiencies and shortcomings better than anyone else. Thus, being able to love yourself despite awareness of your own faults allows you to offer the same affection to others.

A lot of the time we are unable to recognise and accept our own imperfections, let alone forgive them. Perhaps that's why we can't do the same for someone else? In short, if we are unable to consider ourselves worthy of being loved unconditionally, we will never come close to offering others our unconditional love.

2. Make Choices Out of Love

Love is not one-size-fits-all, so try asking yourself, 'What is the most loving thing I can do for this particular person at this particular moment?' For instance, if you have two friends who are dealing with the loss of a loved one, one may welcome a shoulder to cry on and someone to talk to them to share their grief; the other might prefer to be left alone, needing quiet and solitude instead. If you are not sure what the best way to help someone is, you could simply ask them, 'How can I help you with this right now?' Then act out of love.

3. Forgive the People You Love

"Forgiving is not something we do, but something we are."

– Piero Ferrucci

One of the ways to love someone unconditionally is to forgive them. We often wait, stubbornly, for the other person to apologise; but how about we overcome our ego and go right ahead a forgive them?

There's a famous religious saying: "*Hate the sin, love the sinner.*" The meaning derived from this is that loving someone unconditionally means we may not always agree with what a person does, but it should not affect the way we love them.

This does not mean we allow people to walk all over us, bully us, or otherwise mistreat us in the name of unconditional love. Extricating ourselves from such a hurtful environment is the wise choice. But we can still love the person despite hating their behaviour.

4. Do Not Shield Your Loved Ones from Pain and Discomfort

Unfortunately, pain and discomfort are inevitable in life. None of us can fully escape from sorrow and distress. Viewed in the right way, these hurts are the way we grow and strengthen who we are. Loving someone must not be confused with shielding them from pain and suffering, as hard as that is, for this is the way that they, too, will be able to grow as a person. Helping someone through the bitter experiences of life as well as enjoying the good times also means you get the chance to grow closer to each other.

Of course there are times when we must protect a vulnerable loved one, a child or an elderly parent; but where possible it is not acceptable to lie to protect the feelings of someone we love. Instead, our honesty is a message that says we can work things out together.

5. Love is Acceptance

Caring is an essential part of loving someone in the sense that we are interested in their wellbeing and happiness. However, we don't want to care in the sense that our love is based on specific outcomes, because that's what conditional love is. Our attitude must therefore be, 'I accept what you decide, because I love you regardless of your choices.' This doesn't mean we don't care; it means we accept another's freedom of choice as part of loving them unconditionally.

We are all capable of offering love like this to others. It's not about 'What's in this for me?' or 'I'll love you unconditionally if you love me back,' because that is immediately attaching expectation to the relationship.

To sum up: *don't love because of how someone lives, but simply because they live.*

Chapter 19

Turning Weakness into Strength

"Strength does not come from what you can do. It comes from overcoming the things you once thought you could not."
– Rikki Rogers

Let's begin with the story (source unknown) of a 10-year-old boy who decided to practice judo, despite the fact he had lost his left arm in a car accident.

"The boy started taking lessons with an old Japanese judo master. He was doing well, so he couldn't understand why, after three months of strenuous training and hard work, the master had taught him just one move.

'Master,' the boy finally dared to say, 'don't you think I should be learning more moves?' 'This is the only move you know, but this is the only move you'll ever need to know,' the master replied.

The boy didn't quite understand what the master meant. However, believing in his teacher, the boy focused on the only move his master had taught him. Several months later, the master made the boy participate in his first tournament. Surprising himself, the boy easily won the first two matches.

The third match proved to be quite challenging but, after some time, the opponent became impatient and charged. The boy deftly used his one move and won the match. Still amazed by his success, the boy made it to the finals.

In the finals, his opponent was bigger, stronger and more experienced. It seemed the boy had no chance in winning the final match. Worried that the boy might get injured, the referee called a time-out. He was about to stop the match when the master intervened. 'No,' the master insisted, 'let him continue.'

Soon after the match resumed, the opponent made a critical mistake: he dropped his guard. The boy took advantage of the moment and instantly used his move to pin him. The next thing he knew, he had won the match, and the tournament. He was the champion.

On the way home, the boy and master reflected on the tournament and the final match. Then the boy mustered his courage and asked, 'Master,' he said, 'how did I win the tournament with only one move?' 'You won for two reasons,' the master replied. 'First, you have almost mastered one of the most difficult moves of judo. And second, the only known defence for that move is for your opponent to grip your left arm.'

Thus, the boy's biggest weakness had become his greatest strength."

This may come as a surprise to you, but knowing your weaknesses can help you identify your strengths. It may seem counterintuitive, but knowing your weaknesses helps you become a better person, identify where you are passionate, and where you will be truly successful.

Identifying Personal and Professional Weaknesses

Here's a simple yet great exercise. Take a notebook or piece of paper and create a list of things you consider real weaknesses, both personally and professionally. Make sure you base this on what you are doing in your life right now, rather than focusing on your past experiences or future goals. Are you brave enough to be honest with yourself?

If you suspect you're not, get in touch with someone you trust. Get face-to-face with this person and ask him or her to be brutally honest with you. Have them write their own list, without seeing what you have written down.

It might be hard to take a look at this second list, but it will serve two purposes: it will confirm your observations in the case of similar items on the list; and might expose any illusions you have about yourself in the case of your trusted companion's observations!

Take some time to analyse any surprises or mismatches across the two. Why do you think some of those mismatches showed up? Is it possible that you think certain things are your strengths but, in reality, they are not? Write your thoughts down, alongside each point, and discuss them. Although difficult, this is the perfect way to identify our weaknesses.

How Weaknesses Can Become Strengths

Similar to the young boy at the beginning of this chapter, I know of a child born with Type-II diabetes. As it turns out, he also became a three-time all-American distance runner.

He could blow away most of his competition. Why was that? From what I heard about this young man, whereas some might treat diabetes as a biological weakness, he never complained. He checked his blood before and after every race. He didn't say anything about it. He just went out there and did what it took to be great. You could say that his determination to win against the odds of being born with diabetes became his overriding strength.

Richard Branson, the billionaire we all know, was famously told by one of his schoolmasters that he would either grow up to be a criminal or a millionaire. Add that to the fact that he was dyslexic, apparently lazy, could not read very well, and did not speak very well, and you have the perfect set up for weaknesses running his life. He became a billionaire from building a world-dominating business from scratch. How did he do it? He knew school wasn't his game, and, as a result, he channelled his energy into a game he was interested in, which was entrepreneurship.

Take a look at those two lists again. What is on there that could become the thing that transforms your weakness into your greatest strength?

Conquer Your Fear

Fear of the dark, fear of being alone, fear of heights, fear of the unknown, and fear of not being able to do well in life are some of the common fears people experience. They allow fear to hold them back in life. Fear is their weakness. But identifying your greatest fear, means you can conquer fear.

Erik Weihenmayer became the first blind man to

climb Mount Everest. And not only Everest. He has also climbed the seven highest peaks in the world, one from each continent.

Any one of us could ask how he managed to do that; how he overcame his fear to set foot on the world's highest mountains. Was he perhaps twice as diligent about every single footstep that he took? Was he maybe twice as mentally prepared compared to hundreds of other climbers who attempt to climb Mount Everest and, on occasion, lose their lives doing so? Whatever the case, he went on to do exactly what may have seemed impossible.

Conquering our fear, whatever it is, equips us to take life on from a place of diligence and commitment.

Dealing with Our Weaknesses

Simply put, weakness can either make us succumb, or emerge as a far stronger version of ourselves. Perhaps our weaknesses include a lack of direction, determination. Maybe we don't like trying new things. How can we turn these into strengths?

1. Set Your Goals

Setting yourself goals in overcoming weaknesses gives you the momentum to keep going. It's all about gearing up to make a change in your behaviour. Guilty of a lack of determination? Set a date, today, to either stop a bad habit, or begin a good one. (Better still, start today!) Translate that into other areas of your life, personally and professionally. Make it your life's purpose to be more determined, and set the wheels in motion by setting goals to achieve a certain thing by a certain date.

2. Do the Things You Are Afraid of Doing

This weekend, arrange to do something you've never done before – wall climbing, or asking someone on a date (anything that works for you!) – and notice how you feel before and after the event. Next time that opportunity comes up at work, despite it being out of your usual remit, say yes. Doing things we're afraid of is a surprising experience, as quite often it turns out the fear was totally misplaced, and the sense of achievement far outweighs the original fear.

3. Don't Compare Yourself to Others

There is nothing more debilitating than thinking this person is better than you because they can do so-and-so, or things are easy for that person because they're better looking or more intelligent. You are you, with all your individual good bits and bad bits. Hone in on your strengths. Perhaps you are a great listener, or the one who is always able to calm a difficult situation? But don't compare yourself to anyone. Compare yourself to you, and monitor your progress.

I saw a video on YouTube where a man spoke openly about his OCD and bipolar disorder. It was hard for him to control his emotions, and he'd messed up a lot of relationships. Getting fed up with his life, he forced himself to look at himself and get better control of his actions and words. That new control over his body and mind changed his life. Because of his sessions with psychologists, he grew fond of psychology and was deeply moved by all the depressed people he met. As a result, he dropped out of art college and started a degree in psychology. He's now in his final year. He thanked his depression for the great life he now has. His actual words were: *"I have never been this satisfied and happy before!"*

The greatest way to turn a weakness into a strength is to challenge it, and yourself, head on. It can be the blessing in disguise; the very thing that changes your behaviour, and your life.

Chapter 20

Build a Legacy

"The greatest legacy one can pass on to one's children and grandchildren is not money or other material things accumulated in one's life, but rather a legacy of character and faith."

– Billy Graham

As Billy Graham says, the legacy we leave goes beyond money or possessions, it is much more about who and what we were. Should it be important to us that people remember our character and behaviour rather than how much money we earned, or how new our car was? It should be if we want to shape our behaviour into something people recall with fondness and respect.

We all want to feel that our life mattered, and it is possible to start deciding what our legacy will be from this very moment. It's never too late to start building a 'character' legacy, adopting behaviour that will be remembered long after we have departed this life. Consider the following:

- Start living today the way you want other people to remember you.

- Take a look at how you use your resources and time. Could more be invested in character rather than possessions?
- Deciding what you want your legacy to be can influence every decision you make, and affect every interaction you have.
- Gaining clarity on your legacy can give your life new purpose and meaning.

There are several ways in which we can identify the legacy we want to leave behind. Let's discuss a few now.

1. What Will Your Verse Be?

I'm sure most of you must have seen the film *Dead Poets Society?* Set in 1959 at a fictional elite conservative boarding school located in Vermont, the film stars Robin Williams as John Keating, an English teacher who inspires his students through poetry. There's one scene where Keating talks to his students about the meaning of life. In this scene, Keating quotes from Walt Whitman's poem, 'O Me! O Life!':

"O me! O life! of the questions of these recurring, Of the endless trains of the faithless, of cities fill'd with the foolish [...] what good amid these, O me, O life?"

And Keating answers: *"That you are here. That life exists, and identity; that the powerful play goes on, and you may contribute a verse."*

The poem discusses life as being like a play, in which you get to contribute a verse. Keating then asks the students, *"What will your verse be?"*

The verse that you contribute to the play of life will become your legacy.

2. Imagine Yourself as a Relay Runner

In a relay race, members of a team take turns running with a baton in their hand, passing it to the next runner. This is exactly how Barack Obama saw his life:

"I saw myself as a relay runner. I would take the baton and I would run my leg of the race. And then I'd pass the baton to someone else [...] Each generation tries to make progress knowing that what we do is not going to be perfect [...] But, hopefully, we've run our leg of the race effectively – and the world's gotten a little bit better."

The questions we need to ask ourselves are: How well am I doing on my leg of the race? Am I preparing to pass the baton to someone else? What is my baton? Asking these thought-provoking questions helps us identify the legacy we want to leave behind.

3. Picture Your Funeral or 80th Birthday Party

This is a very helpful exercise known as the 'obituary exercise'. It might seem a little macabre, but it's actually incredibly useful when creating our legacy. Ask yourself these questions:

- What will my family and close friends miss about me the most?
- What positive attributes will they associate me with?
- How will they describe me to the next generation?

If this is a little too scary, picture your 80th birthday instead. (It's a variation of the exercise that works equally well.) Ask these questions:

- What would I like the people in attendance to say about me?
- Do I think they're being polite, or speaking from the heart?
- Based on my behaviour, will they regard me with utmost respect, or mere tolerance?
- How we answer to these questions will certainly encourage us to take a long, hard look at ourselves and the character legacy we will leave behind.

4. What Will be Etched on Your Tombstone?

Here's a great example of just that. Before dying, Thomas Jefferson, the third president of the United States, gave specific instructions on what he wanted on his tombstone. Jefferson demanded there be an obelisk with the following engraved on it:

"Here was buried Thomas Jefferson, author of the declaration of American Independence, of the statute of Virginia for religious freedom, & Father of the University of Virginia."

The chances are most of us won't have something as great and iconic as Thomas Jefferson on our tombstones, as it's highly likely we are going to live far more ordinary lives. However, the point is that we need to live our lives with grace, and strong values, so that these qualities can make an important difference in the lives of others. So, think about it: What words do you want to be etched on your tombstone? Once you decide that, your life's pursuit is to live up to those words.

5. Further Questions

Benjamin Franklin said, *"If you would not be forgotten as soon as you are dead, either write something worth reading or do something worth writing."*

Not many of us get to write a book, but it's interesting to consider whether we do anything worth writing about. Take a look at these 10 questions. They might help you to decide just what it is you want people to write or say about you:

1. What do you want your life to stand for?
2. How do you want to be remembered by your family and friends?
3. What will those beyond your circle of family and friends remember you for?
4. Whose lives do you want to touch?
5. What kind of impact do you want to leave on your community?
6. Will the world be a better place because you were in it?
7. What contributions do you want to make to your field?
8. What lessons would you like to pass on to future generations?
9. What do you want to leave behind in terms of a model to follow?
10. How can you best serve that model?

These simple questions really do help in deciding the path we need to walk now.

Different Ways to Leave a Great Legacy

Ray Bradbury wrote in his famous book *Fahrenheit 451*:

"Everyone must leave something behind when he dies. A child or a book or a painting or a house or a wall built or a pair of shoes made. Or a garden planted. Something your hand touched some way...and when people look at that tree or that flower you planted, you're there."

The following might help to jump-start your legacy ideas:

1. Try to add knowledge to the field you work in, or contribute something to make it better than before.
2. Work hard and show perseverance and commitment in all of your projects.
3. Pour your experiences, feelings and thoughts into a diary, or even a book, highlighting the poignant moments and lessons learnt.
4. If you are able, leaving money can serve as a foundation upon which family and/or friends can build a business or whatever is important for their future.
5. Donate money to charities that work for a cause you deeply care about.
6. Write down family traditions and recipes which can be passed on to the next generation and the generation after that.
7. Set an example by serving as a good role model in society, involved in good causes such as fundraising for a new playground, or a garden in a care home.

8. Pass down a family heirloom.
9. Mentor someone and transfer your strong work ethic or values.
10. Do some volunteer work. Really give of your time and care.
11. Start a non-profit organisation or a business that is geared towards improving the lives of other people.
12. Record video messages for your loved ones, or create a scrapbook for them. Maybe even create a website, or write a blog.
13. Endow a scholarship to your alma mater for future students.
14. Write letters that reveal your life lessons, hopes and values. Think of it as an emotional heirloom.
15. Pass down handmade items with strong sentimental value.
16. Pass down skills and know-how in your specialist field.
17. Right a wrong.

The legacy we leave is not just in our possessions, but in the quality of our connections and how we spend our time. The greatest waste on earth, which cannot be recycled, is the waste of time.

Robert Baden-Powell, a British army officer and writer, said,

"Try and leave this world a little better than you found it; and when your turn comes to die, you can die happy in feeling that, at any rate, you have not wasted your time but have done your best."

And Maya Angelou said,

"People will forget what you said, people will forget what you did, but people will never forget how you made them feel."

What a beautiful statement. Our greatest legacy should be how we made people feel when they were in our company. Were they happy? Safe? It's through our behaviour not our possessions that we have the power to answer yes to these vital questions, and leave a legacy of care and support and love.

Chapter 21
CPR and You

"Take some time to learn first aid and CPR.
It saves lives, and it works."
– Bobby Sherman

Imagine you are standing at a bus stop, or in your local supermarket, or even travelling on a plane, and suddenly someone goes into cardiac arrest and falls to the floor, clutching their chest and close to unconsciousness. Now imagine standing there not being able to do anything, gripped by helplessness as this person fights for their life, and then slides into unconsciousness before your eyes.

The survival chances for cardiac arrest is doubled, even tripled, if immediate cardiac pulmonary resuscitation (CPR) is administered in the time waiting for the emergency services to arrive. As someone willing to be the best they can be in this life, learning CPR is an absolute demonstration of that commitment.

What Does CPR Do?

Some estimates state that for every minute without CPR, a person's survival chances go down by about 10 percent. That means that after around 10 minutes, survival is close to zero.

If we were the one in cardiac arrest, wouldn't we hope, and pray, that one of the people around us knew how to perform CPR? Be that person who learns.

The aim of CPR is to circulate the blood, and subsequently vital oxygen, to the brain and other organs. Without this, survival chances are greatly diminished. Even if a person is taking an occasional gasp for air, immediate CPR can mean the difference between life and death.

Kids and CPR

More and more kids are being trained to perform CPR. Through the efforts being put in by different institutions, it is said more than one million students every year learn how to perform CPR.

It's simply not true that children cannot learn to perform CPR just as effectively as adults, which is why different medical organisations have taken the initiative to visit schools and teach kids and their teachers how to administer this life-saving care.

The British Heart Foundation shared the experience of a woman named Emily, who has been teaching CPR to her year 7, 8 and 9 students for years. She knows exactly how important it is for young people to learn this life-saving skill.

According to Emily, *"When you see somebody come back to life, after you have performed CPR on them, you get a feeling that does not go away. It's a feeling that you always remember. Always, always remember! Performing CPR on somebody who is seconds away from dying gives you that belief that, actually, we can do something to save the person's life. We can help people."*

According to Emily, people are more concerned about not knowing what to do than ever before. One of her students, Sarah, was in year 9 when she did her first aid training, not realising she would need those skills in real life when her father collapsed.

Emily is incredibly proud of her student.

"*Most weekends I'm teaching first aid, and I always, always talk about Sarah,*" she said. "*People don't think it will happen to them. But you do not need to be a doctor or a paramedic to save somebody's life. Anybody can do it.*

Reasons You Should Learn CPR

"The most common reason many people die from cardiac arrest is because no one nearby knew CPR, or if they did know it, they didn't do it properly."

– Michael Sayre

None of us know when we might encounter a situation where someone's life is dependent on CPR; and once we are trained to perform CPR, we have the most wonderful gift we could ever give someone at our disposal: their life. If you are a little unsure about the procedure, here are a few reasons that might convince you to learn this life-saving skill:

1. CPR is Easy to Learn

It does not take years of medical training to learn CPR. In fact, it often takes just a single class to learn the technique. You can also learn how to perform it with the help of online videos. However, it's better to attend a proper class so that you have a chance to ask some questions and ensure your technique is correct.

2. CPR Increases Chances of Survival

Cardiac arrest can end a life in a matter of minutes. Once the heart stops beating, it prevents oxygen from getting to the brain, which can have a devastating effect in a very short period of time. Performing CPR provides that oxygen to the brain, and other important organs, and gives the patient a much greater chance of recovery.

3. CPR Increases Confidence

Facing a medical emergency can be a terrifying experience for anyone, especially for those who are not trained to step in and offer some medical help. CPR training will provide you with not only the valuable skills and knowledge necessary to save a dying person's life, but the confidence to do so.

4. CPR at Home

Did you know that almost 70 percent of sudden cardiac arrests occur at home? Therefore, the odds are you might need to use your CPR skills to help someone really close to you.

It's a fairly common misconception that sudden cardiac arrests happen only to the elderly or sick. The truth is that anyone can go into cardiac arrest as a result of heart abnormalities, or external causes like drowning, trauma, drug overdose or electrocution, to name but a few. Other medical causes, such as inflammation of the heart muscle due to an infection, can also lead to sudden cardiac arrest. That means children and teens as well. There are no age specifics when it comes to who can succumb to cardiac arrest and, as stated before, children and teenagers can also learn CPR. New parents might also wish to learn infant and child CPR.

Everyone hopes tragedy will never strike; but hope is not a strategy. Cardiac arrest does not come with a warning; it can strike unexpectedly and to the most unexpected of people. Understanding this simple fact is a step towards deciding to step up and learn CPR. Encourage your children, your spouse, your work colleagues and your friends to learn. Make sure caregivers have learned. Some would say it's our moral duty to do so.

"I hoped I would never have to put my CPR skills to use, but when a 12-year-old collapsed because of cardiac arrest, I was thankful to know exactly what to do. She's here today, alive and healthy, thanks to my lifesaving CPR training."

– FROM A STRANGER WHO SAVED A GIRL'S LIFE

That stranger could be you.

Conclusion

We have discussed a lot here, and I hope some of it has resonated with you. We are all responsible for who and what we are, and how we come across in our interactions with others; and we are all able to change our behaviour and become the master of those interactions, without ego or judgement, just the desire to be the best we can be.

By way of summary, let's take a brief look at some final elements that support the undeniable truth that the only behaviour we control, in any situation is, our own.

Don't Sweat the Small Stuff

Often we allow ourselves to get all worked up about things that, upon closer examination, aren't really that big a deal. A driver, for example, might cut in front of us in traffic, and rather than let it go and get on with our day, we turn it into a drama, playing out an imaginary confrontation in our mind had we had the opportunity to tell the driver what we thought of them. Many of us may even tell other people about the incident! Having compassion for the driver – perhaps he was late, or super-stressed? – means we can maintain our demeanour, and brush this small annoyance off with no further thought.

There are innumerable examples we could use to illustrate the point – having to wait longer than we hoped in the supermarket queue, someone bumping into us in the street, being on hold to our electricity supplier for what seems like for ever – but sweating this small stuff does us no good, and creates personal stress and transmutes stress onto those around us. It also means we completely lose out on the chance to be that kinder, gentler and better version of ourselves.

Accept That Life Isn't Always Fair

Recognising this sobering fact can be very liberating, as we immediately lose our need to complain about life's injustices, wallowing in self-pity if things don't go our way, or throwing the towel in and giving up.

'*It's not fair*!' is something a five-year-old screeches when they can't have what they want; it's certainly not the attitude for someone intent on accepting life head on, ups and downs and all, and learning from it.

Surrendering to this fact has helped me raise two children with the right attitude towards fairness and instilling this truth in them, in practical decisions about who to help in their times of crisis – it's a tough call, but some really do create their own bad situations; others do not – and with my own personal struggles at times, when I've felt I've been 'unfairly' treated.

Accepting that life doesn't seem very fair at times

helps us to avoid unnecessary self-pity. Pity is such a self-defeating emotion, and it achieves nothing except bring everyone around us down to our level. Rise above. See the opportunity in a situation that hasn't quite worked out as we hoped – whether a relationship or a business deal, for instance – and see the lesson. The next time you find yourself thinking about the injustices that come your way, try reminding yourself of this. You'll be surprised how it nudges you into action, rather than dumping you in a hole of doom and gloom.

Practice Random Acts of Kindness

There is no prescription for how to practice random kindness; but it must come from the heart. It might be to pick up litter in your neighbourhood, make an anonymous contribution to a charity, send some cash in an unmarked envelope to someone experiencing genuine financial distress, or save an animal by taking it to an animal rescue agency. We can do one or all of these things, and more, depending on our time and circumstances.

There is huge contentment to be enjoyed each time we do even small things to make another person's life easier in service of kindness. But never give to receive. Just give.

Let Others Be Right

There is a very famous notion often quoted by philosophers and psychologists: *"You can be right, or you can be happy."* Which would you prefer?

Being right, defending our position, takes an

enormous amount of mental energy and often alienates us from the people in our lives. Conversely, the need to make other people wrong encourages them to become defensive. It also creates anger and damages relationships. Some people, consciously or unconsciously, believe it's their job to show others how their positions, statements and points of view are incorrect, and that, in doing so, the person they are correcting is going to somehow appreciate it, or at least learn something.

Has anyone you know ever thanked you (or even agreed with you) when you've insisted on correcting them just to make yourself 'right' at their expense?

It's not that it's never appropriate to be right when certain circumstances arise. But there are ways of expressing ourselves, as we've discussed. Discretely pointing out a spelling error in a colleague's email to a client is one thing; making a loud verbal display about your superior skills, in front of the whole office, is entirely another. On other occasions, such as a moral or cultural debate, we can learn to express an opinion without the need to be 'right'. Those who are in the habit of communicating with others in a 'I am right and you are wrong' manner are often resented and avoided.

A wonderful, heartfelt strategy for becoming more peaceful in our exchanges is to let others have their say without needing to prove anything in return. They may absolutely feel they are right with respect to a certain matter or moral stance. Let them. When someone says, 'I really feel it's important to...' rather than jumping in and saying, 'No, it's far more important to...' or any of the dozens of other forms of conversational bullying, simply let it go and allow their statement to stand. Doing this allows us to discover the joy of participating in and witnessing other people's happiness, which is far more rewarding than a battle of egos. We don't have to sacrifice our deepest philosophical truths, or most heartfelt opinions, but, starting today, let others be right, and stay happy.

The Snowball Effect of Overthinking the Bad Stuff

Have you ever noticed how uptight you feel when you're caught up in thinking about someone who was rude to you, or that guy who cut you up at the traffic lights? One thought leads to another, and yet another, until, at some point, you become incredibly agitated.

You might wake up in the middle of the night and remember a phone call that needs to be made the following day. Then, rather than feeling relieved that you remembered such an important call, you start rehearsing that call, getting into a state about how the result might not go your way. Pretty soon you're thinking, *I can't believe how busy I am. I must make fifty phone calls a day. Whose life is this anyway? My boss's or mine?* and on and on until you're snowballing into a row with your boss, and what you're going to tell him about his life and your life…

We're all guilty of this kind of thought attack; this debilitating mental rehearsal for the bad stuff – that most likely won't even happen. Needless to say, it's impossible to feel peaceful with your head full of this kind of overthinking going on.

The solution is to notice what's happening before

your thoughts build any momentum, because the sooner you catch yourself in the act of building your mental snowball, the easier it is to stop. So instead of chasing that single thought about tomorrow's phone call, commit it to memory, grateful that you remembered, and don't follow it up with another. It takes practice, but you'll be amazed how effective this simple exercise can be in halting that snowball, night or day.

Live in the Present Moment

To a large degree, the measure of our peace of mind is determined by how much we are able to live in the present moment. Irrespective of what happened yesterday or last year, and what may or may not happen tomorrow, the present is where we are – always.

Without question, many of us have mastered the neurotic art of spending much of our lives worrying about past problems, and playing out future problems, so much so that we end up anxious, frustrated, depressed and confused. Conversely, we also postpone our happiness, convincing ourselves that some other day will be better than today, that we'll be happy when this happens or that changes. Unfortunately, the same mental dynamics that tell us to look toward to the future often keep us there, and we miss out being happy right now. John Lennon once said, "*Life is what's happening to you while we're busy making other plans.*" While we're busy making "*other plans*" our children are busy growing up, the people we love are moving away or growing older and dying, and our bodies are getting out of shape. In short, we're missing out on the amazing life happening in every present moment. I know it's been overused, but life is not a 'dress rehearsal' for some later date. Now is the only time we have, and the only time we have any control over.

Mark Twain said, "*I have been through some terrible things in my life, some of which actually happened.*" I don't think I can say it any better than that!

When our attention is in the present moment, we push fear, anxiety and procrastination from our minds. We choose to live now, where it's all happening. There is no greater mantra for life, and no greater way to keep ourselves on track to being the best we can be in every present moment. It keeps us committed to a life and a legacy of good, moral and upbuilding behaviour that accepts and embraces all of our experiences and encounters as the amazing lessons they are. And most important of all, it frees us from the need to control or change those we get to spend this precious thing called life with.